ANTOINETTE SIBLEY

**Distributed By
Princeton Book Co. Publishers
P.O. Box 109, Princeton, NJ 08540**

ANTOINETTE SIBLEY

Photographs by
LESLIE E. SPATT

Text by
MARY CLARKE

Introduction by
SIR FREDERICK ASHTON,
O.M., C.H., C.B.E.

DANCE BOOKS 9 CECIL COURT LONDON

First published 1981 by Dance Books Ltd.,
9 Cecil Court, London WC2N 4EZ

Printed by BAS Printers Ltd.,
Over Wallop, Stockbridge, Hampshire.

ISBN 0 903102 64 1

Book design by Karen Bowen

All photographs by Leslie E. Spatt,
except the following:

Roy Round, 1, 12 (top two), 13
Houston Rogers, 10, 11 (top)
Edward Griffiths, 11 (bottom)
Rosemary Winckley, 22

*I*t is the very greatest pleasure in looking through this delightful book to be reminded and have recalled before one the singular beauty and intensity of Antoinette Sibley's dancing. Mary Clarke with great perception re-creates in words the magic of so many of her great and affecting performances.

I myself always found her a great pleasure to work with; her response to my requirements was immediate, her musicality and her powers of interpretation and passion inspiring. I can only imagine the great pleasure that the perusal of these beautiful photographs by Leslie E. Spatt will give to her countless admirers, as they have delighted and enchanted me.

Antoinette's dancing always gave me great delight, and when she and Anthony Dowell danced together they cast an unforgettable spell. She has always evoked in me the most loving qualities of warmth and devotion much cherished. Beloved Dorabella!

Frederick Ashton

The year 1956 was a momentous one for Britain's national ballet. The Sadler's Wells Ballet had been established at the Royal Opera House, Covent Garden for a decade and its reputation was world wide. But it had no real security. Surveying the situation, and drawing up a careful and characteristically forward looking memorandum, Dame Ninette de Valois, to whom the company owes its very life, came to the conclusion: "the ballet did not exist . . ." She put her case to Viscount Waverley, then Chairman of the Board of Directors of the Royal Opera House, and eventually on "the thirty-first day of October in the fifth Year of Our Reign", 1956, Queen Elizabeth the Second granted the Charter of Incorporation of the Royal Ballet. The future of the Sadler's Wells Ballet, of the smaller Sadler's Wells Theatre Ballet, and of the junior and senior schools, so vital to the companies' continuation, was secure. The Sadler's Wells Ballet became the Royal Ballet; its school the Royal Ballet School. And in 1956 a student from that school entered the Covent Garden company. She was Antoinette Sibley. The date, of course, was coincidental yet I like to think it was also an omen of the future of a dancer who was to become so closely identified with what today we call Royal Ballet style—a ballerina whose whole training (apart from early classes) was at the Sadler's Wells and Royal Ballet School. And a dancer whose career will ever be associated with the Royal Ballet and the Royal repertory.

Although Sibley did not join the company until 1956, ballet people were already aware of her. I remember while she was still at White Lodge, the junior school, being told by a teacher "we think we have a little Aurora". And there was a matinée of *The Sleeping Beauty* when I made my way along the back of the Stalls Circle, thronged with White Lodgers in their green school uniforms, and among them was an excited buzz. In those days even the tiniest roles were listed in the programme and these students were not interested in that afternoon's Aurora or her prince: "Antoinette Sibley is a Lilac Fairy attendant!" That was the cause of excitement.

Once a member of the company she was soon noticed in small roles—one of Swanilda's friends in *Coppélia*, even as Red Riding Hood in *The Sleeping Beauty*—but the real classical potential showed when she danced the Fairy of the Crystal Fountain on May 3, 1958. Joan Lawson in *The Dancing Times* wrote of her "lyrical qualities and beautifully flowing line". At Christmas that year she danced the Fairy Summer in *Cinderella* with joyous freedom and a wonderful, languourous warmth in the solo. Two of her greatest attributes were already apparent; the essential classicism and the glamourous, sensual execution of movement which would infuse so many roles and culminate, eventually, in her creation of Manon.

On March 21, 1959 the Royal Ballet School gave the first of its matinées at Covent Garden. Today we take these (always joyful) occasions very much for granted but in 1959 it seemed a gigantic undertaking for the School to dance *Coppélia* on the stage of the Royal Opera House. Dame Ninette, of course, knew that they were ready but felt they also needed just a little help from recent graduates who had stage experience. She cast Sibley as Swanilda, Graham Usher as Franz and

Lambert Cox as Dr Coppelius. Thus Sibley earned another place in the Royal Ballet's history, acquitting herself most happily. Dame Ninette made a curtain speech about the progress of the School (it was originally her school) since Lilian Baylis had given it a home at Sadler's Wells Theatre in 1931, and then reminded the students firmly that they owed everything to their teachers: Barbara Fewster, Errol Addison, Peggy van Praagh, Ursula Moreton, Harold Turner and Pamela May. It was a debt Sibley acknowledged throughout her career: in fact, she said it was Barbara Fewster (now Ballet Principal of the School) who first told her in class that she really was "a beautiful dancer". Those teachers formed her, together with Ailne Phillips and Harjis Plucis, but all through her dancing life she was seeking guidance from older mentors. Not the least of Sibley's gifts was her willingness and ability always to learn.

It was during 1959 that I had opportunities of watching her at work with one of the greatest ballerinas of this century, Tamara Karsavina. Karsavina was writing a series of articles on classical technique, which she called *The Flow of Movement*, for *The Dancing Times* and Sibley consented to pose for the illustrations, demonstrating not only the correct way of performing an exercise but also showing, by distortion, common faults. She posed Sibley for the photographs while I scribbled down some of the words of wisdom which she then incorporated into the articles. Karsavina was then in her late seventies but she preserved still her eloquent instep and her turn out. She used, frequently, to demonstrate what she wanted. Wearing soft black and scarlet slippers, that allowed complete freedom of the foot, she would do some of the little steps of batterie at the barre while Sibley watched and marvelled. I think it was during battement frappé that the most touching event of all the sessions occurred. "To get the full benefit from battements frappés we must train our muscles to give a quick reaction. This means that the dégagé must be sharp and in the nature of a 'hit out'." Sibley tried; Karsavina corrected and then "showed". Sibley's eyes suddenly filled with tears and she embraced her teacher saying "Oh Madame, I can never do it like that."

The friendship established during these working sessions was cemented over small supper parties. One evening Karsavina showed us the mime scene of Giselle's mother and such was the intensity and dramatic power of her gestures and her wonderful eyes that she brought terror into a London restaurant. Thereafter I lost contact with Sibley the person, for my concern was to be with Sibley the ballerina, but I believe she turned constantly to Karsavina for help and advice and Karsavina followed her career with affection.

By the summer of 1959 Sibley had danced the ballerina role in *Ballet Imperial* with an imperial bearing and the grandeur that was to crown her interpretations of the great classics. On October 24, 1959 came the first, unexpected *Swan Lake* at Covent Garden. Partnered by Michael Somes, who was to become her first husband and who was to guide her whole career, she triumphed. After the performance dressing room number four, the size of a small bathroom, was crowded with eight press men, five photographers, innumerable well wishers. The publicity was fantastic but the challenge severe. After the first performance, as Karsavina said, must come "the ripening of the intellect".

Tours to America and to Russia brought Sibley further recognition. Dancing with Graham Usher, she won the heart of the Moscow audience but Natalia Roslavleva, writing in *The Ballet Annual*, observed "Youthful charm, good technique and engaging personalities do part of the work for these dancers. To become great they will have to invest a lot of sweat and tears in the development of mature stagecraft." Usher, alas, did not live to fulfill his promise but Sibley despite constant setbacks due to ill health or injury, confirmed the faith of teachers, mentors, and audiences alike and went on to enjoy a career that was rich not only in interpretations of the classic repertory but also in created roles and in roles which are part of the Royal Ballet's own heritage.

Sibley's first Aurora—predicted so long ago—did not actually happen until December 27, 1961 and she danced with John Gilpin who was making some quietly distinguished guest appearances with the company. About that performance I wrote that perhaps one day Gilpin would be proud of having shared Sibley's debut (once again, she had to go on at short notice) and I also said "Her Aurora, already enchanting, promises to be for her generation what Fonteyn's had been to mine". And I think, now, that it was.

Successfully launched into both the classic and the company repertory, Sibley had yet to find a partner with gifts equal to her own or a choreographer who would fully reveal her very individual dance personality—those "qualities you do not know you possess". In 1964, she found both.

Ashton's choreographic condensation of Shakespeare's play which he called *The Dream* had its first performance on April 2 as part of the Royal Ballet's celebration of the quatercentenary of Shakespeare's birth. He cast Sibley as Titania and Anthony Dowell, a younger dancer just coming into prominence, as Oberon. Singly and together both dancers created magical beings: Ashton used Sibley's speed and lightness in her solo dances, her ease in quick changes of direction, and her girlish sense of fun in her dance with Bottom. But it was in the final great pas de deux that Ashton fused the two bodies and made them aware of how much, through dance, they could give to each other. *The Dream* holds its place in the Royal repertory in its own right but as David Vaughan has observed, it is also "sure of a place in contempory ballet history if only because it initiated a new partnership, Sibley and Dowell, that was to become second only to that of Fonteyn and Nureyev in popular esteem . . . " And he went on to say that although other dancers have taken these roles "no-one has managed to emulate Sibley's swiftness and her impersonation of a half-wild creature, nor the silken fluidity of Dowell's phrasing."

It was in *The Dream* that Sibley and Dowell made their first great impact together in New York and for both of them it must have seemed a magic talisman. In the whole galaxy of shared performances that was to follow nothing was quite so personal to them. And most of all, I think, to Sibley who, probably, was more aware of the honour done to her by Ashton. Steeped by then more deeply in the Ashton repertory than was Dowell she also understood how Ashton could involve his dancers in the creation of a new ballet. "With Fred you are persuaded you are creating it together."

The Sibley-Dowell partnership has already been chronicled, in photographs by Leslie Spatt and a text by Nicholas Dromgoole in *Sibley and Dowell* (London, 1976).

Suffice it here to say it encompassed unforgettable performances in MacMillan's *Romeo and Juliet*; in the great classics, *Swan Lake*, *The Sleeping Beauty*, *Giselle*; in Ashton's *Cinderella*, *Symphonic Variations*, and *Daphnis and Chloë*; in Robbins's *Dances at a Gathering* and *Afternoon of a Faun*; in Ashton's *Thaïs* pas de deux (which remained their own), and finally MacMillan's *Manon* in which the mature Sibley blossomed from childish innocence into a creature of extraordinary sensual allure. (This allure was most vividly evident in her creation of Friday's Child in *Jazz Calendar*, where she and Rudolf Nureyev, by their passion and feeling, made this dance the best in the ballet.) Sibley's Manon, in the first scene, like her Chloë, achieved what Arnold Haskell has described as "the very essence of youth—a quality that it is almost impossible for the very young dancer, pre-occupied with technique to capture".

The quality had also been evident in another creation for Ashton, that of Dora Penny (Dorabella) in *Enigma Variations*. In this character and in her adorable, slightly "stuttering" solo, Ashton seemed to sum up the very essence of all that was most loveable about Antoinette Sibley. When she decided to retire from the stage I wrote that there would be other Swan Queens and other Auroras "but there will never be another Dorabella".

Sibley's decision to retire came after months of struggle to regain strength after an injury. She knew that if she made a come-back she must be absolutely sure of herself, able to sustain her old repertory, able to give young balletgoers, who had perhaps only glimpsed her, performances worthy of their adoration. Wisely, very wisely, she decided to obey the precept of Karsavina: "leave the stage before the stage leaves you". She put a happy marriage and motherhood first. But her allegiance to the Royal Ballet remains total—not only to her old company but to her old school. One phase of Sibley's Royal Ballet career has ended but another one could be beginning.

How best may we sum up Sibley's way of dance? I think of her essentially as a Petipa and an Ashton dancer. She had the grandeur and the classic style for Petipa and came nearer than any other Royal Ballet dancer to the Russian manner: supremely in *Beauty* and *La Bayadère*. In the Ashton ballets, she had the English lyric style which he developed out of the Petipa heritage and she had the warmth, the intimacy, the generosity and love that he poured into his characters. Remembering, so vividly, the radiance that informed her dancing I think of some lines from a ballad by Sir John Suckling:

> But oh, she dances such a way!
> No sun upon an Easter-day
>   Is half so fine a sight.

EARLY ROLES

Opposite, right and top left, *Coppélia*, with Graham Usher.
Opposite, bottom left, *Ballet Imperial*, with Pirmin Trecu.
Above, *Napoli*, with Georgina Parkinson, Brian Shaw, Lynn Seymour, Graham Usher and Merle Park.
Right, *Ballet Imperial*, with Desmond Doyle.

EARLY ROLES

Opposite, top left, *Le Baiser de la Fée*.
Top right, *Two Pigeons*.
Bottom, Peasant pas de deux from *Giselle* with Michael Coleman.

Right, *La Fille mal Gardée*.
Below, *Two Pigeons*.
Bottom, *Sleeping Beauty* with Ray Barra (Stuttgart Ballet).

ROMEO AND JULIET

Top left, with Gerd Larsen.
Below, with Anthony Dowell.

ROMEO AND JULIET
With Anthony Dowell

ROMEO AND JULIET

With Anthony Dowell

ROMEO AND JULIET

With Anthony Dowell

22

Opposite
LILAC GARDEN

With Anthony Dowell.

Right and below
SCÈNES
DE BALLET

SCÈNES DE BALLET

Below, with Michael Coleman, David Gayle, Kenneth Mason and David Drew.
Opposite, right and below, with Michael Coleman.

25

GISELLE

With Anthony Dowell

GISELLE

Opposite, with Vergie Derman and Gerd Larsen.
Above, with Anthony Dowell.
Right, with Vergie Derman.

GISELLE

With Anthony Dowell and Gerd Larsen.

GISELLE

With Anthony Dowell

GISELLE

With Anthony Dowell

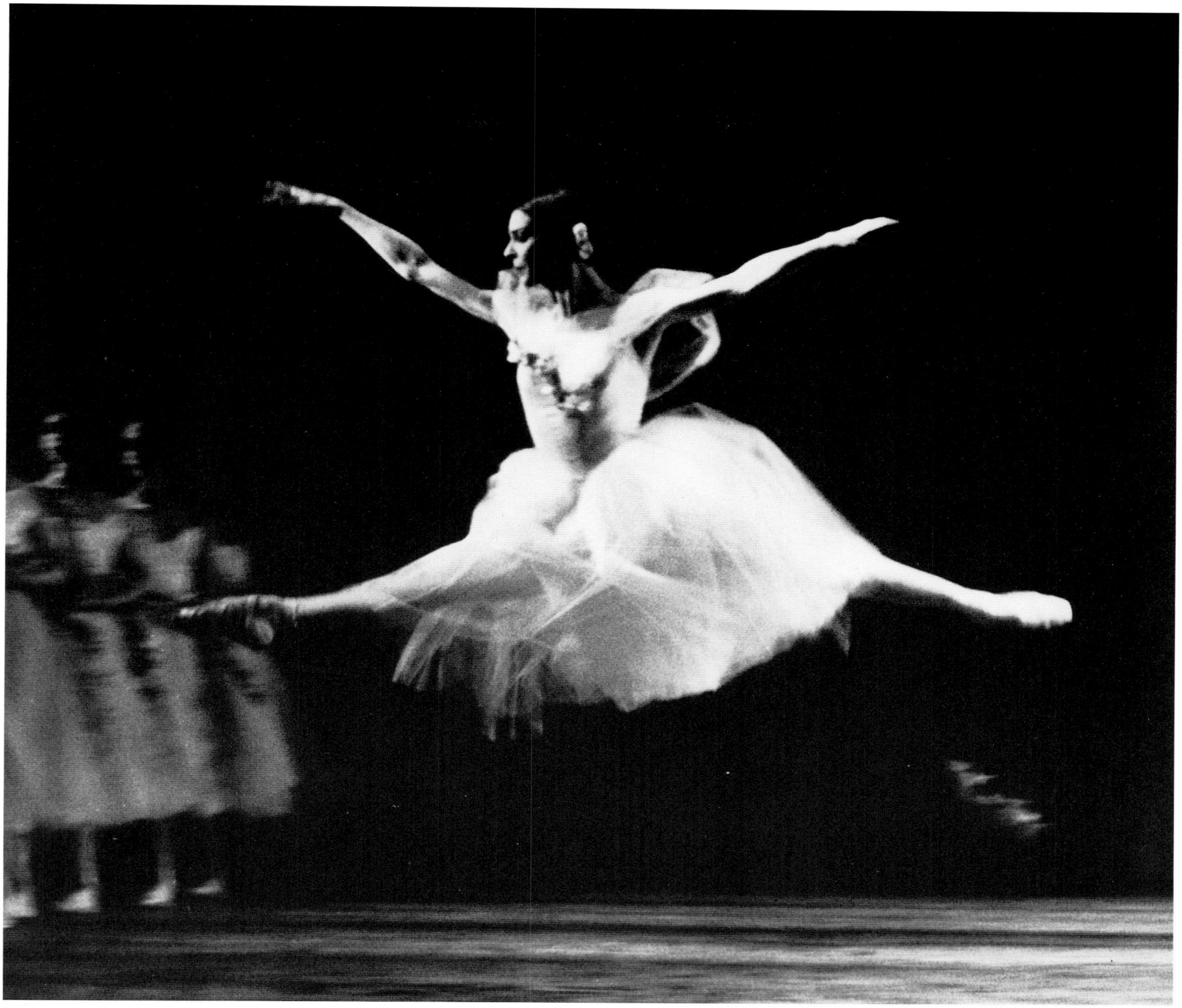

GISELLE

With Mikhail Baryshnikov

JAZZ CALENDAR

With Rudolf Nureyev

FLOWER FESTIVAL
AT GENZANO

With Alain Dubreuil

Opposite
FAÇADE

39

DAPHNIS AND CHLOË

Left, with Anthony Dowell.
Below, with Anthony Dowell and John Craxton.
Right, with Anthony Dowell, David Drew and Robert Jude.

41

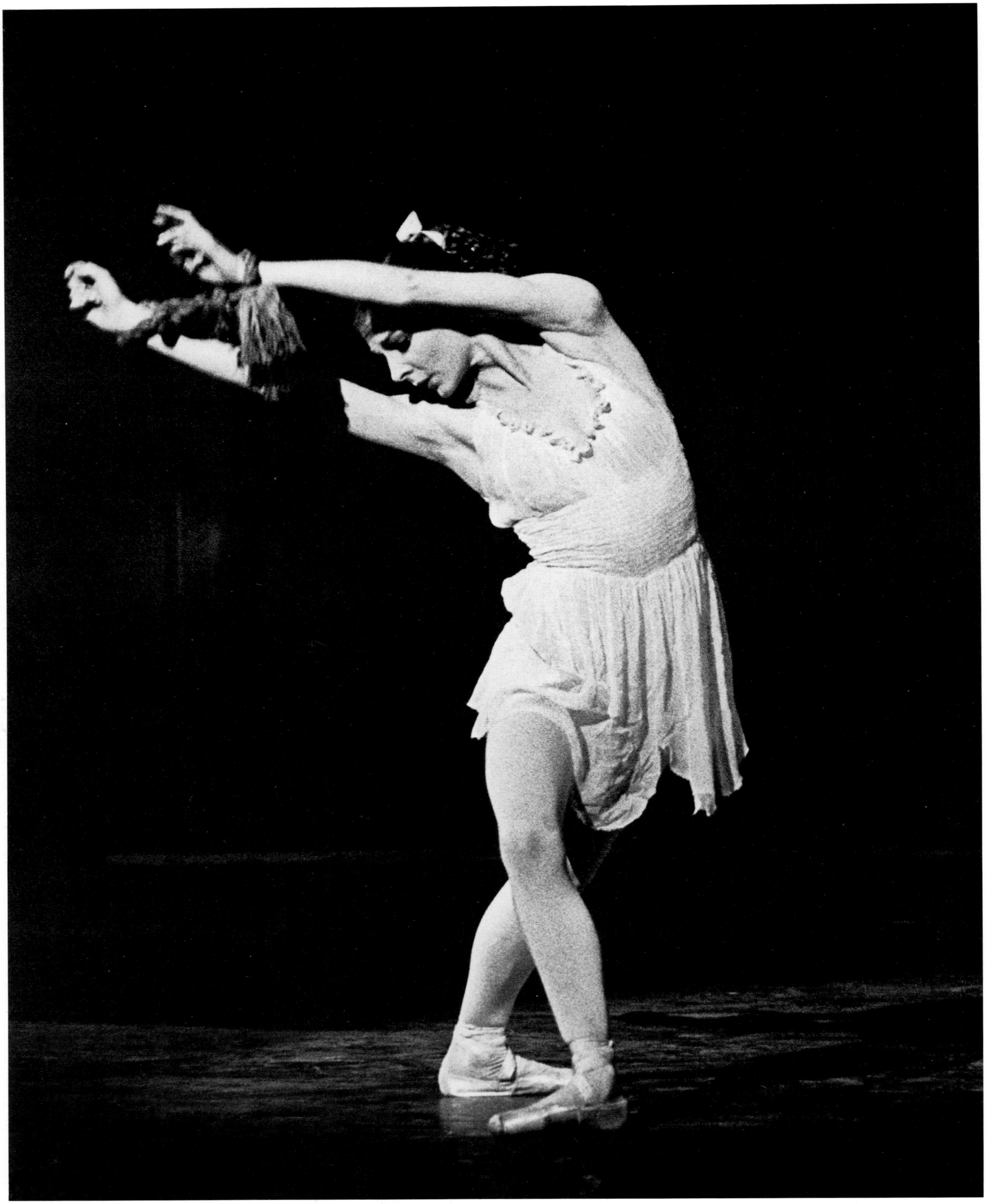

DAPHNIS
AND CHLOË

DAPHNIS AND CHLOË

With Anthony Dowell

45

DAPHNIS AND CHLOË

With Anthony Dowell

OFFSTAGE

FIREBIRD

Top right, with David Wall

48

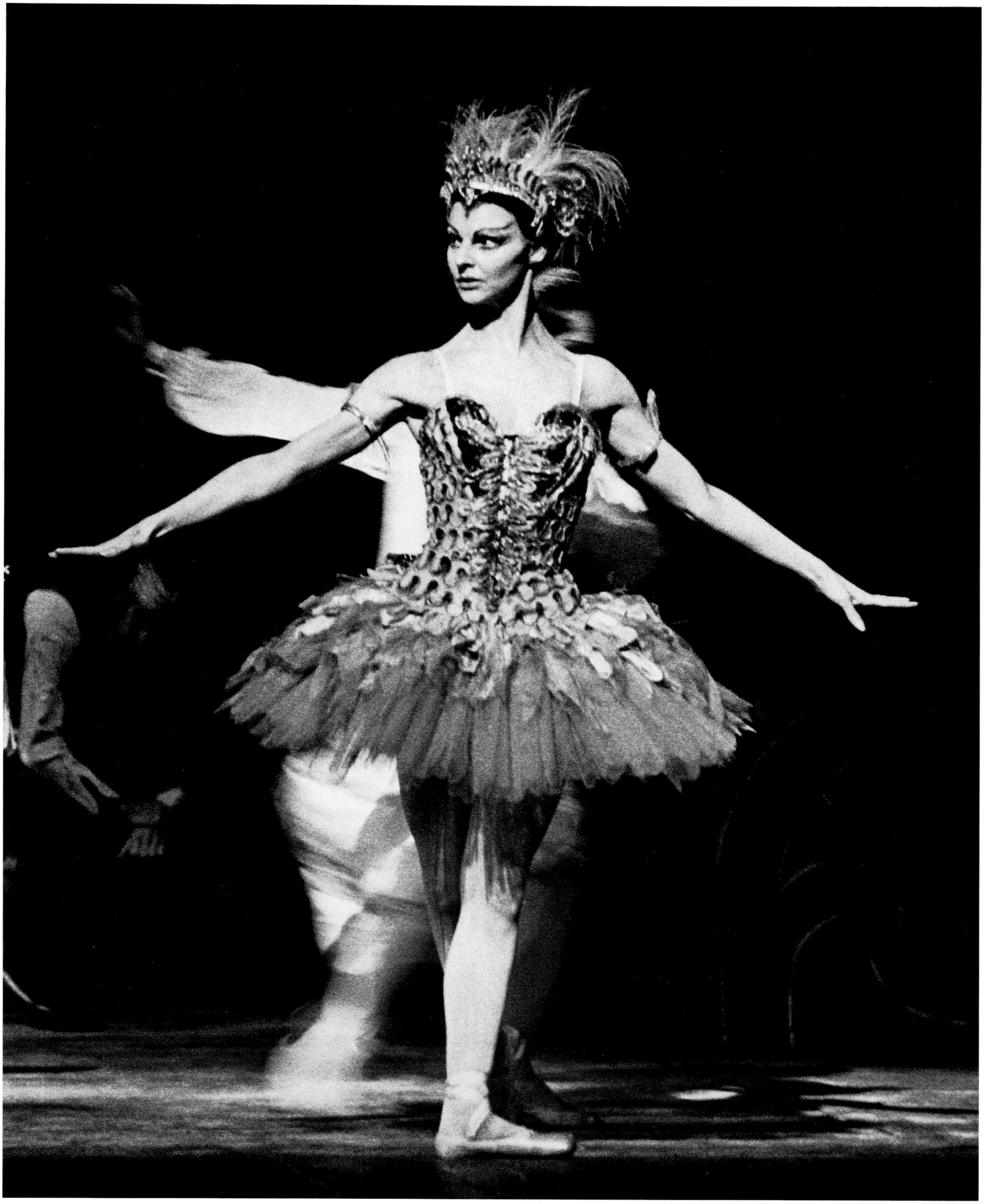

SWAN LAKE

With Anthony Dowell

51

SWAN LAKE

With Anthony Dowell

53

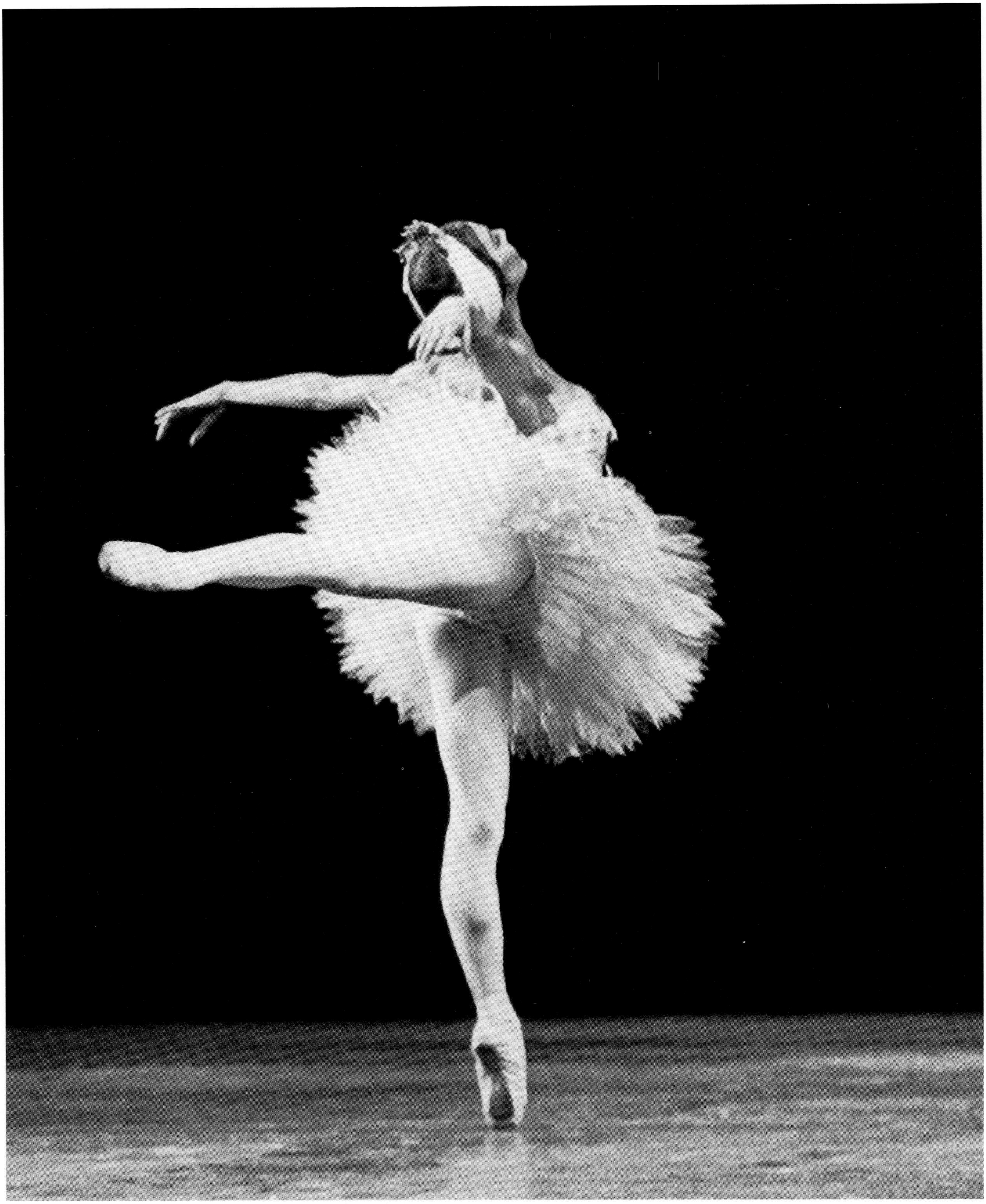

SWAN LAKE

With Anthony Dowell

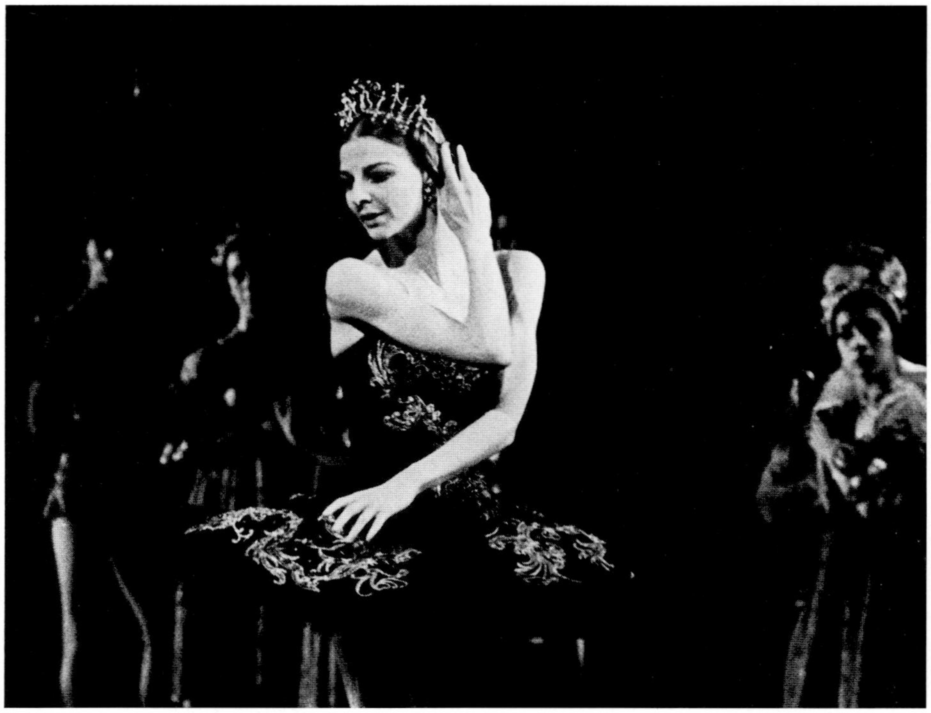

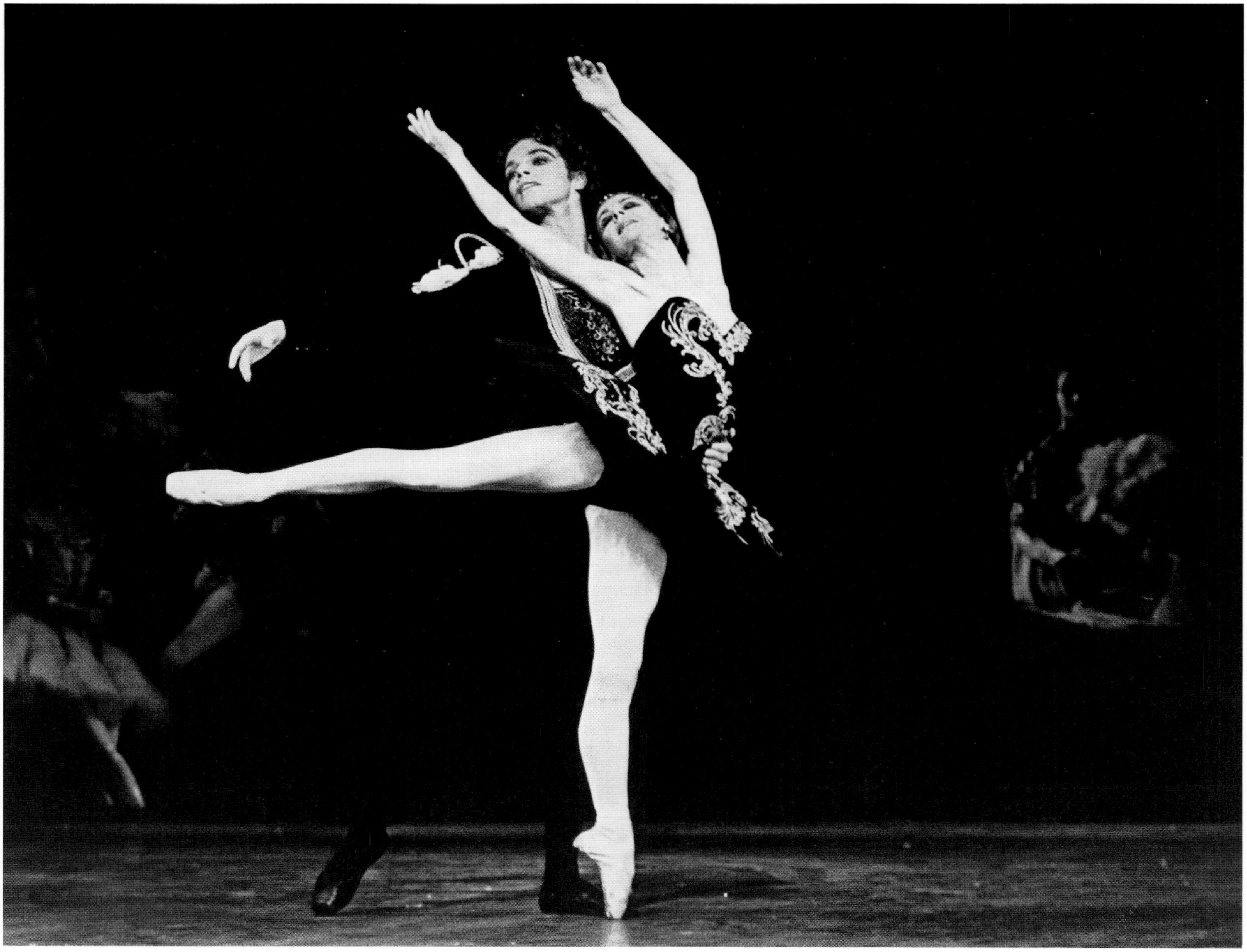

SWAN LAKE

With Anthony Dowell

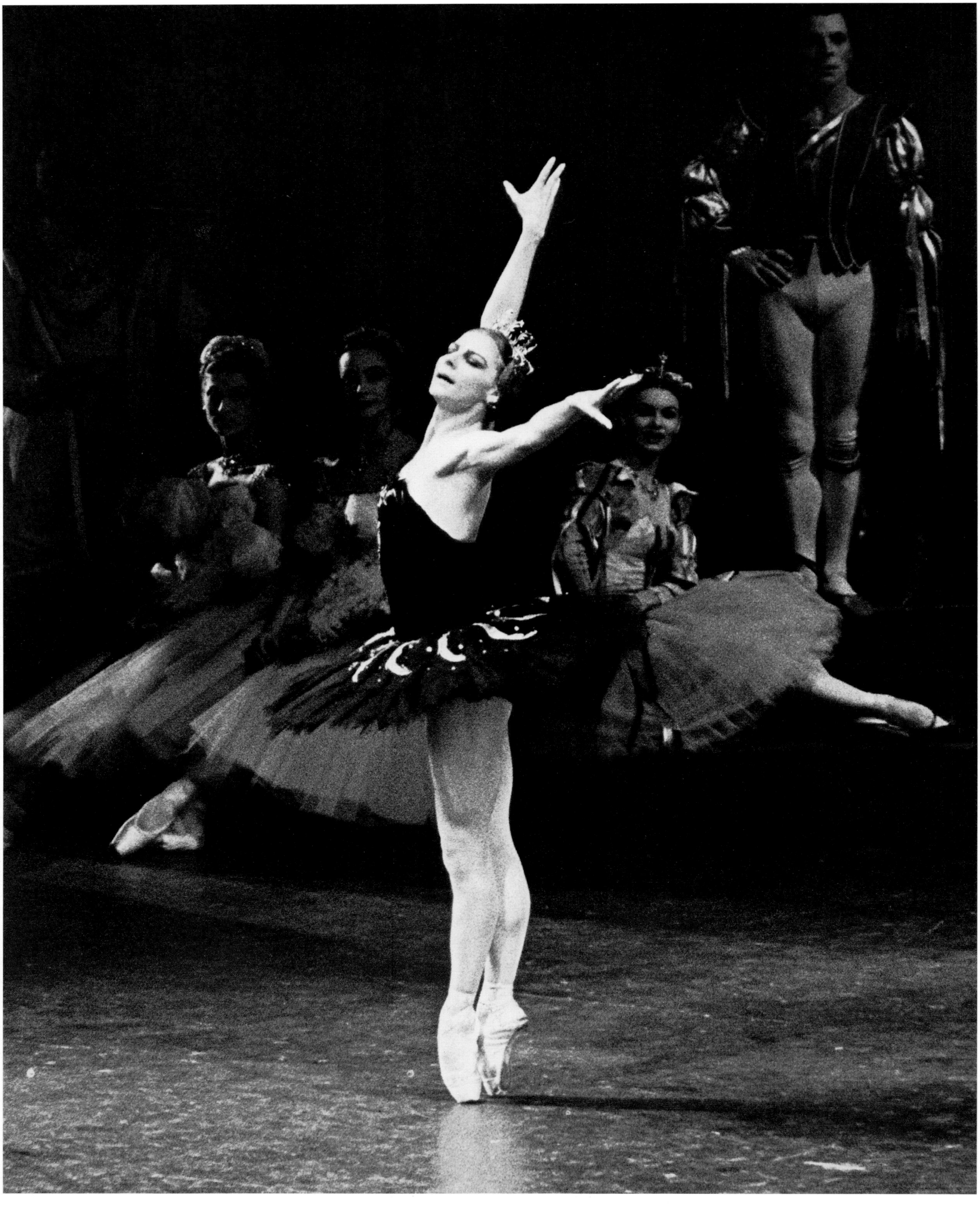

SWAN LAKE

With Anthony Dowell

60

SWAN LAKE

With Anthony Dowell

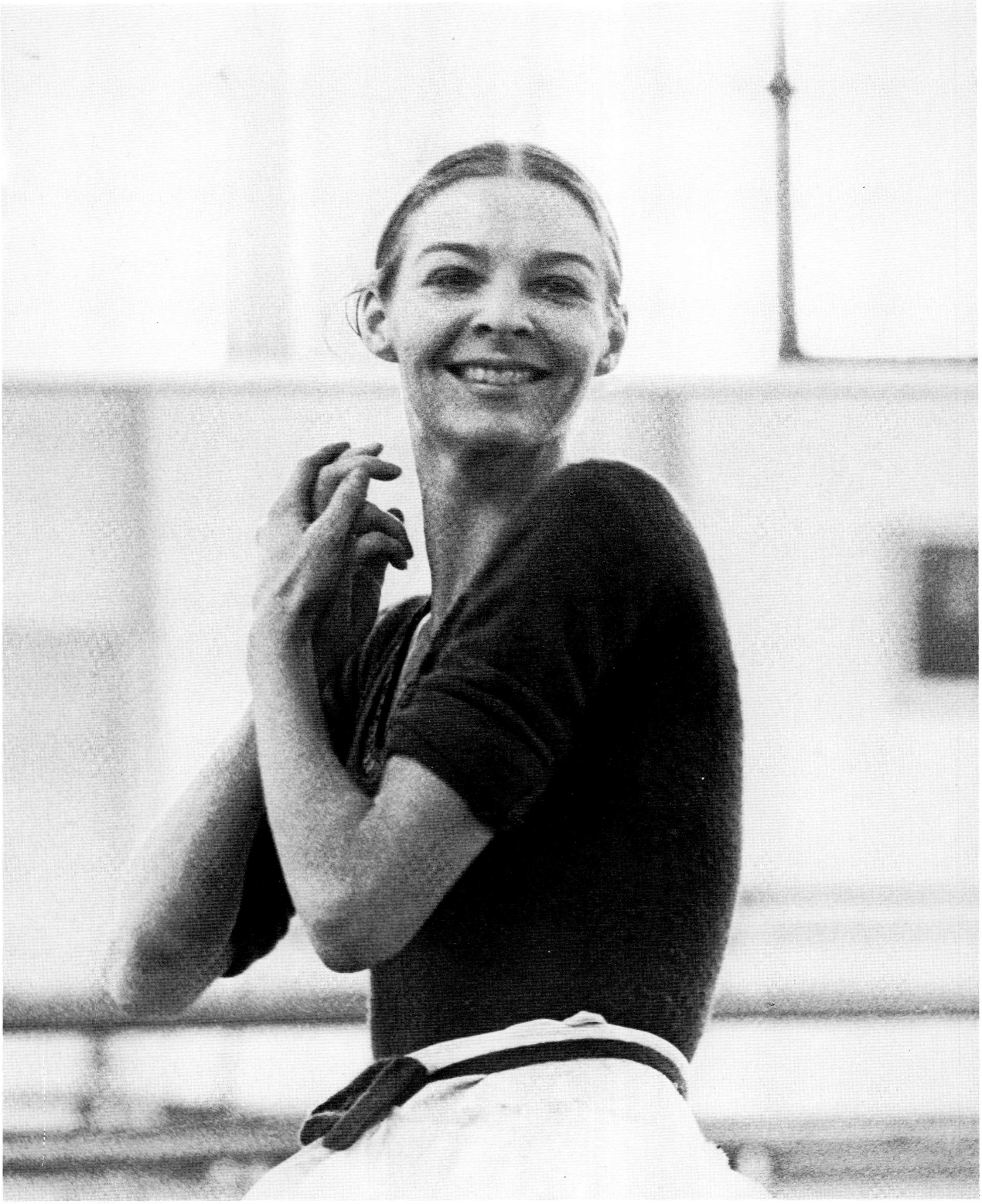

REHEARSAL

With Anthony Dowell for *The Dream*.

REHEARSAL

Opposite, with Michael Somes for *Giselle*.
Below, with Anthony Dowell for *Giselle*.

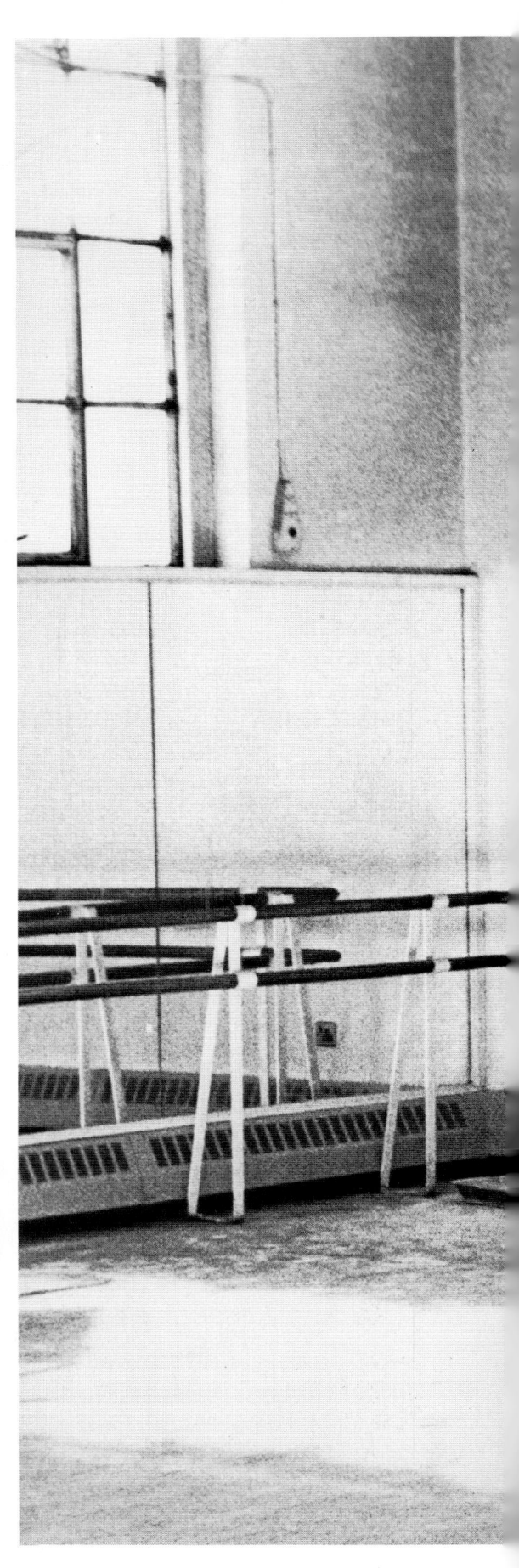

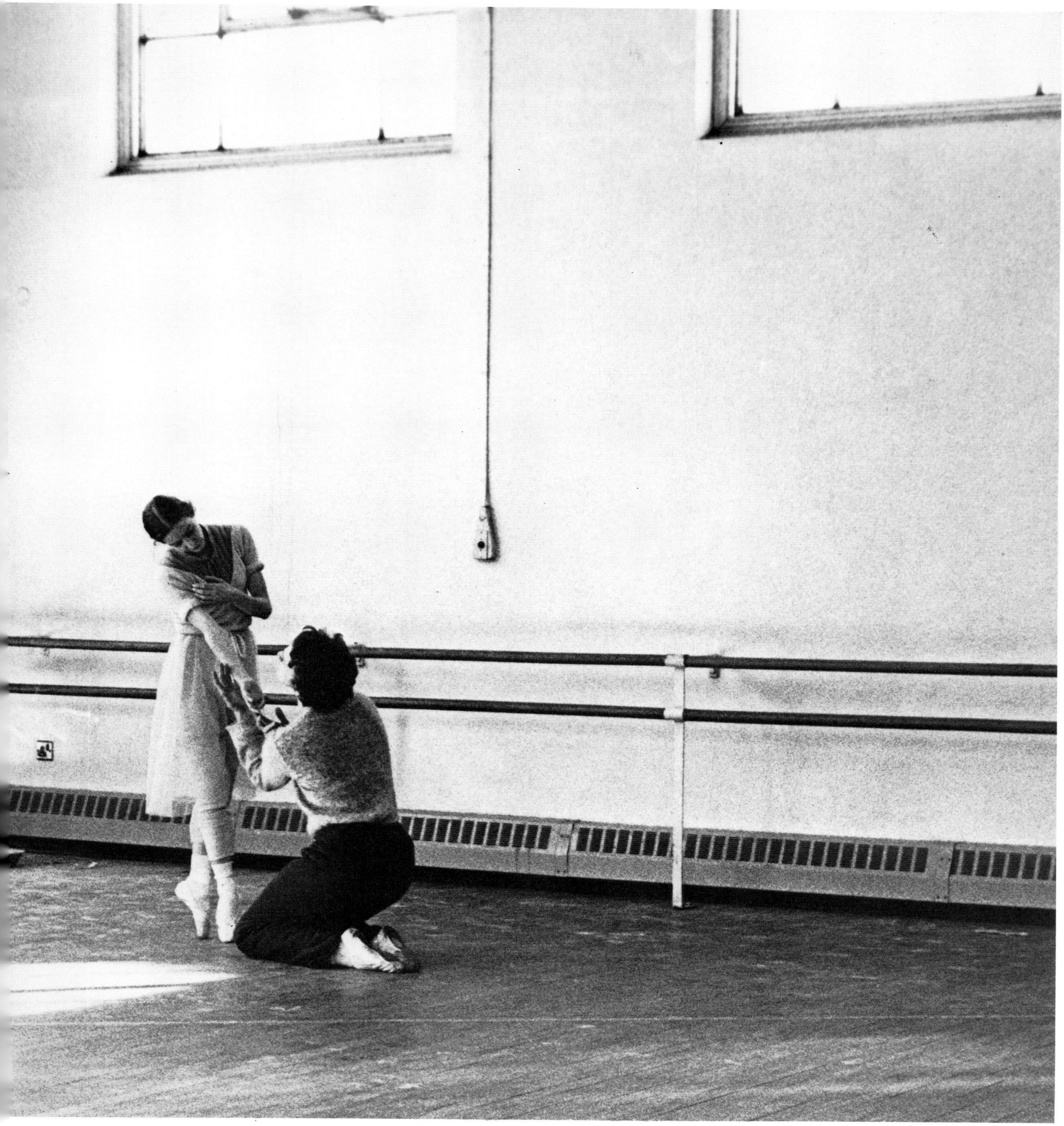

REHEARSAL

Left, with David Drew.
Opposite, with Anthony Dowell for *Thaïs*.

67

68

TRIAD

With Anthony Dowell and Wayne Eagling

TRIAD

With Anthony Dowell

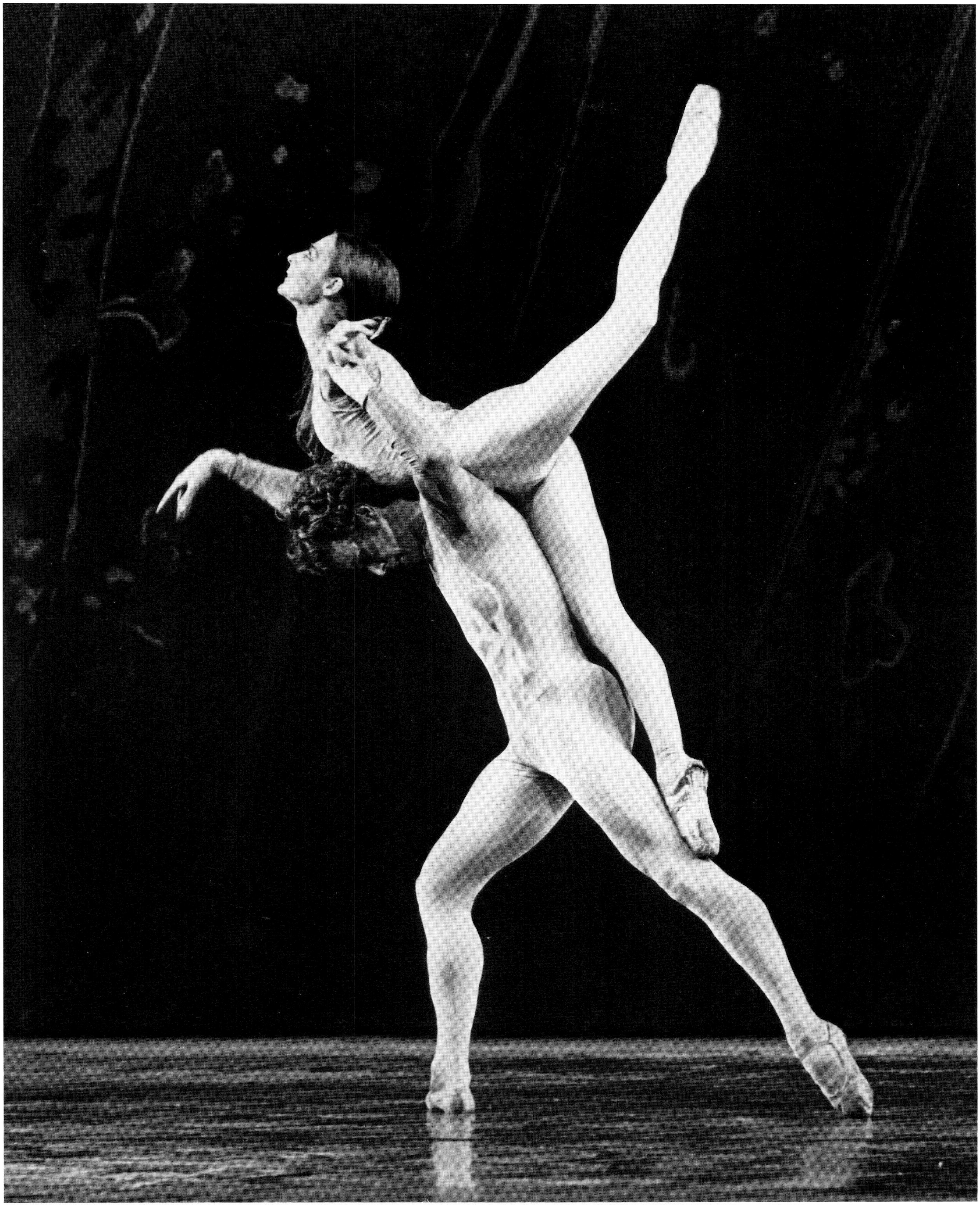

72

LA BAYADÈRE

Opposite, with Rudolf Nureyev.
Above, with Michael Coleman.

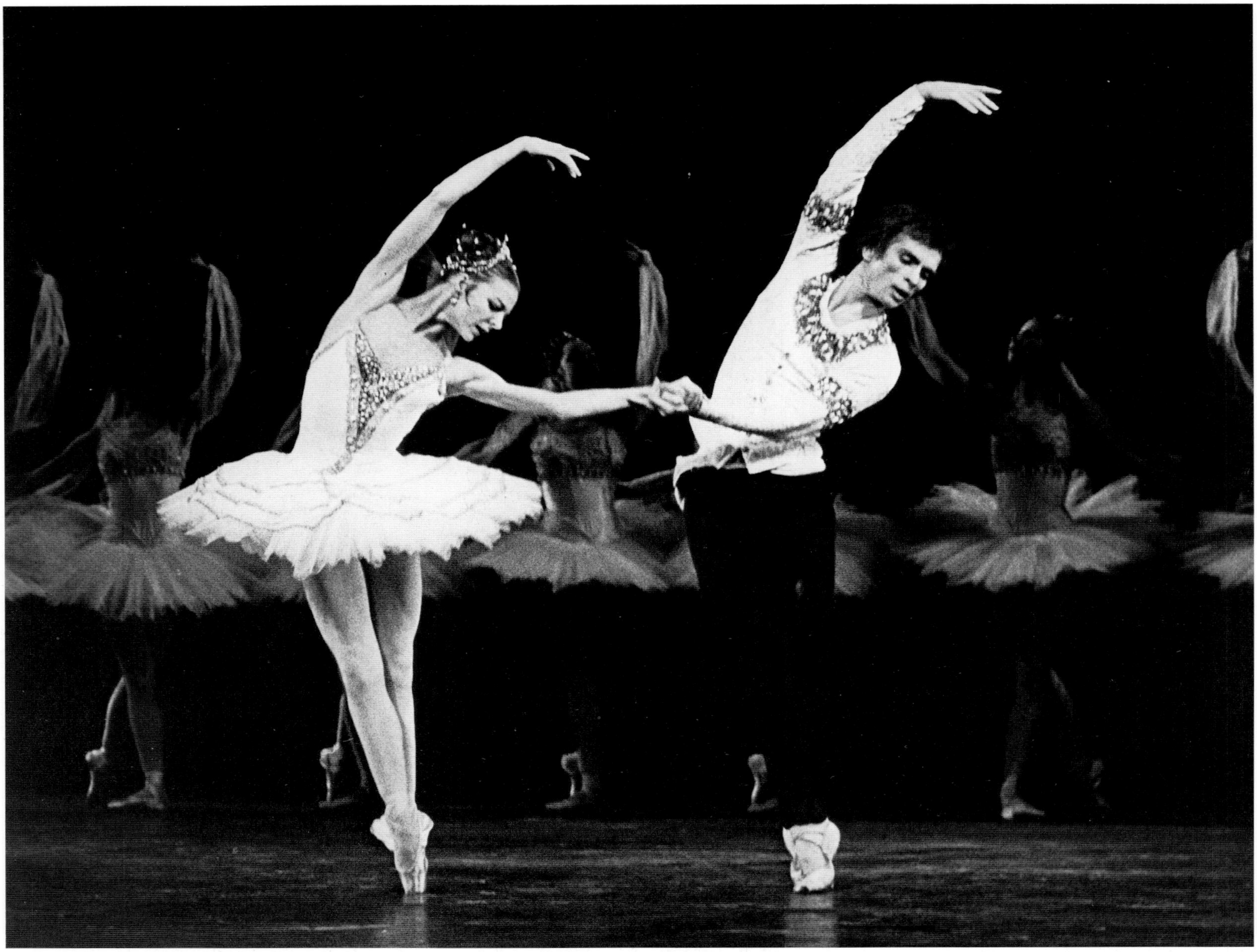

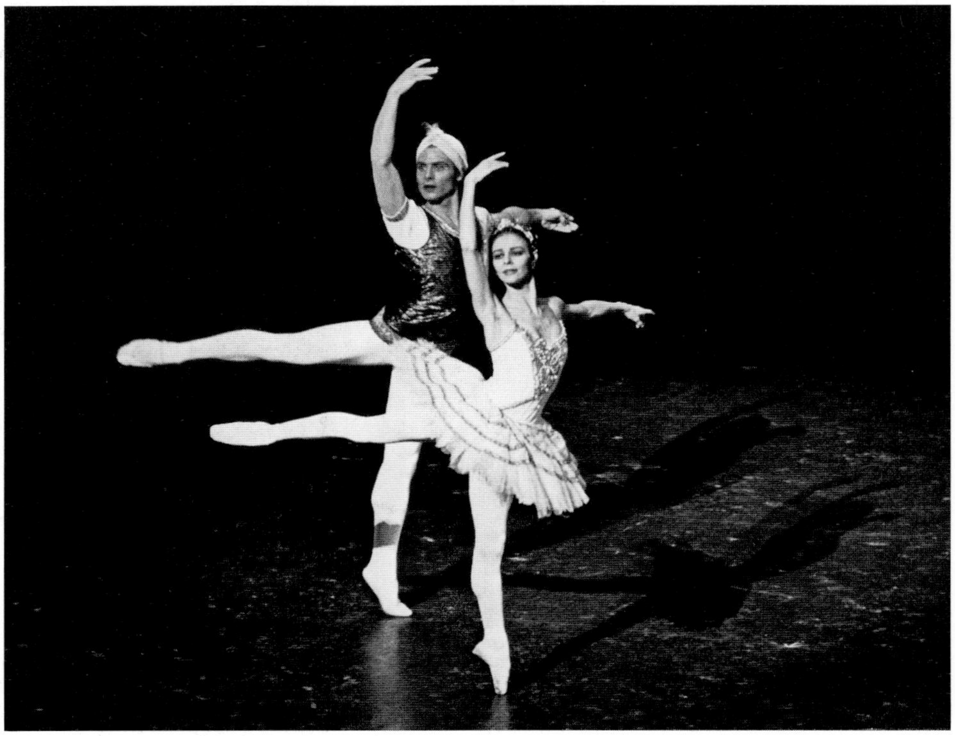

LA BAYADÈRE

Opposite top, with Rudolf Nureyev.
Opposite bottom, with David Wall.
Right, with Anthony Dowell.
Below, with Michael Coleman.

76

THE DREAM

With Anthony Dowell

78

SONG OF THE EARTH

Opposite bottom, with Anthony Dowell.
Right, with Lesley Collier.

80

ENIGMA VARIATIONS

With Derek Rencher

82

Opposite
RAYMONDA

With Anthony Dowell

Right
PAVANE

With Anthony Dowell

83

84

CINDERELLA

Above, with Sir Frederick Ashton

86

CINDERELLA

With Anthony Dowell.
Below, with Anthony Dowell and
Alexander Grant.

CINDERELLA

With Anthony Dowell.
Opposite, with Sir Frederick Ashton and Sir Robert Helpmann

89

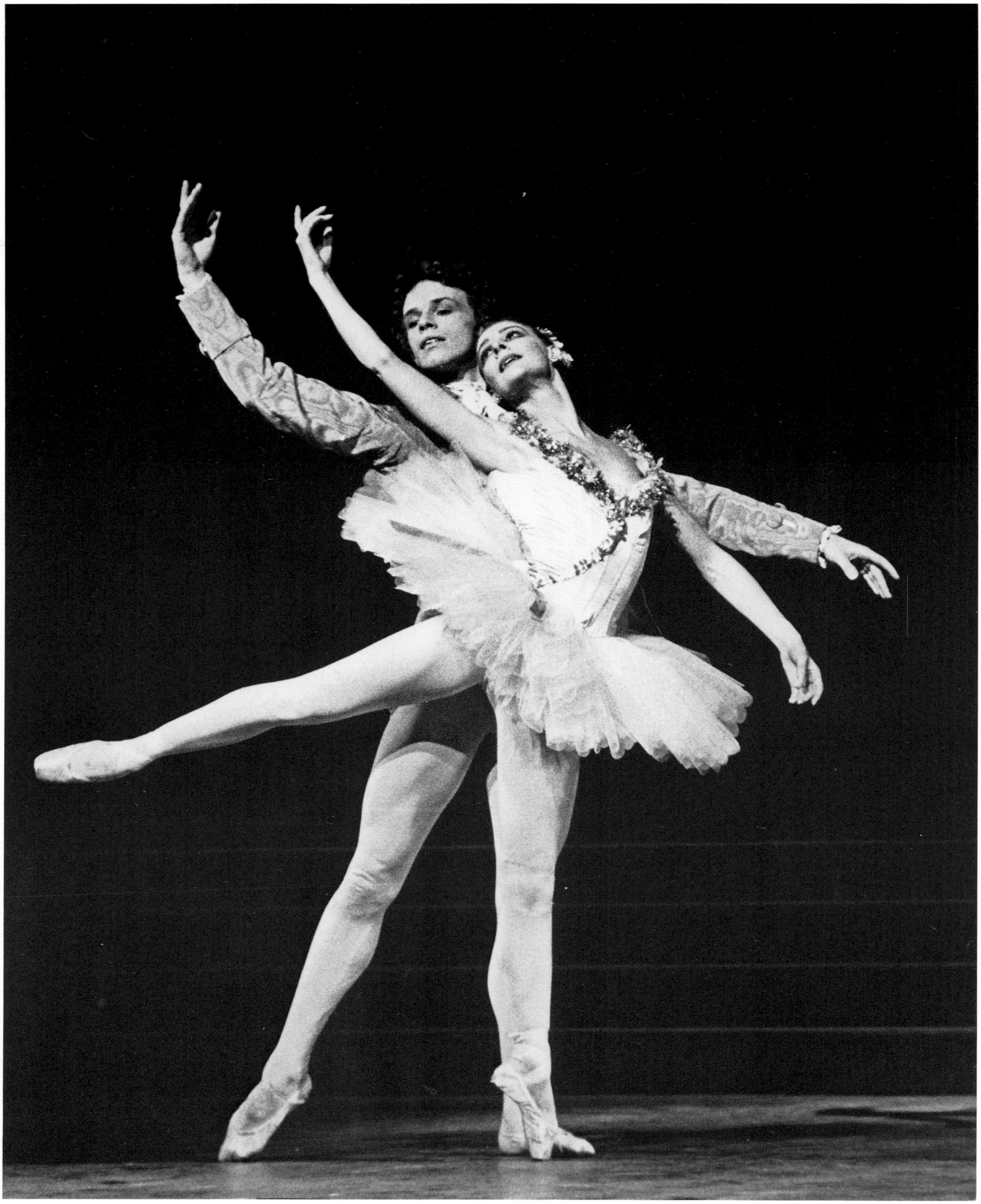

CINDERELLA

With Anthony Dowell

92

Opposite
THE NUTCRACKER

With Anthony Dowell

Right
ANASTASIA

With Anthony Dowell

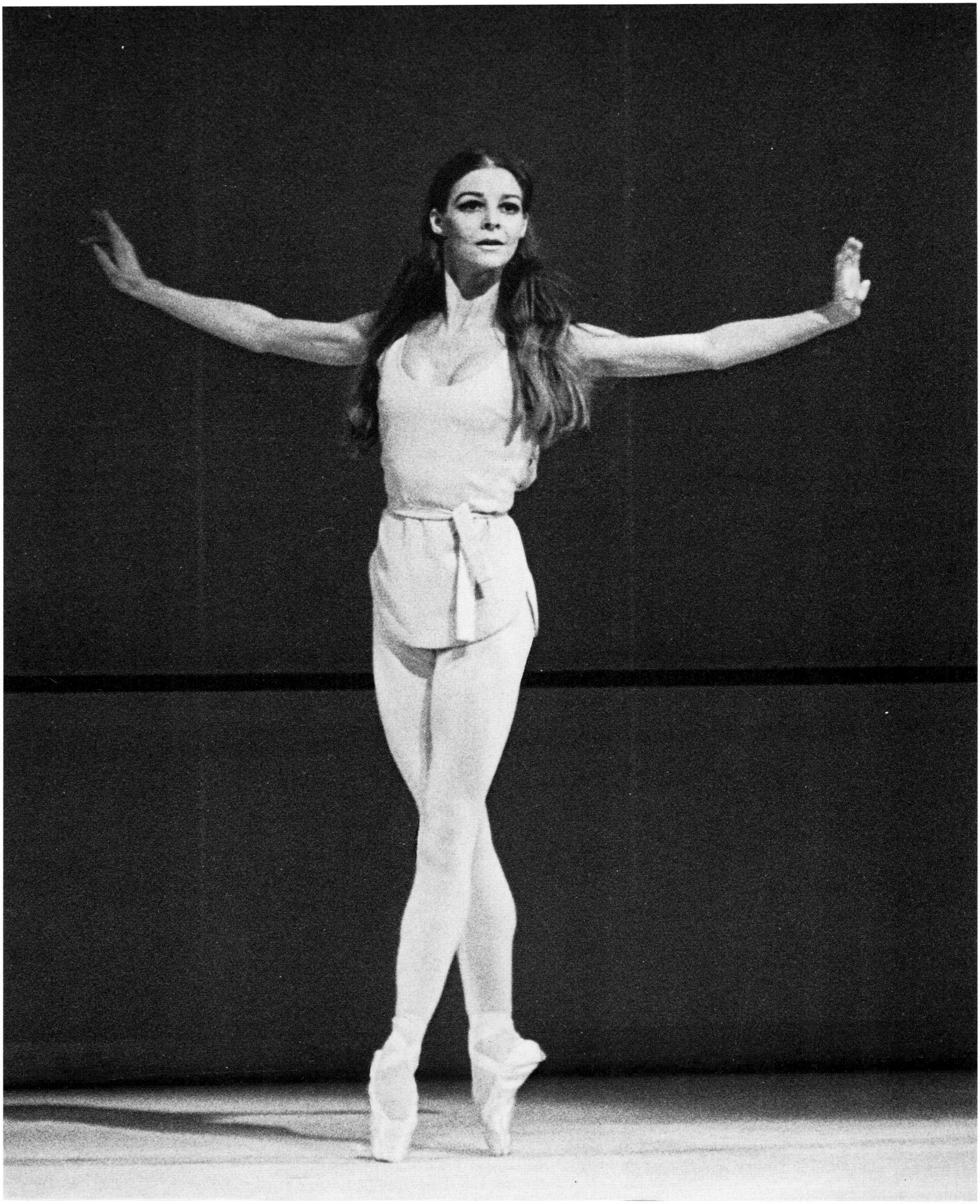

AFTERNOON OF A FAUN

With Anthony Dowell

AFTERNOON OF A FAUN

With Anthony Dowell

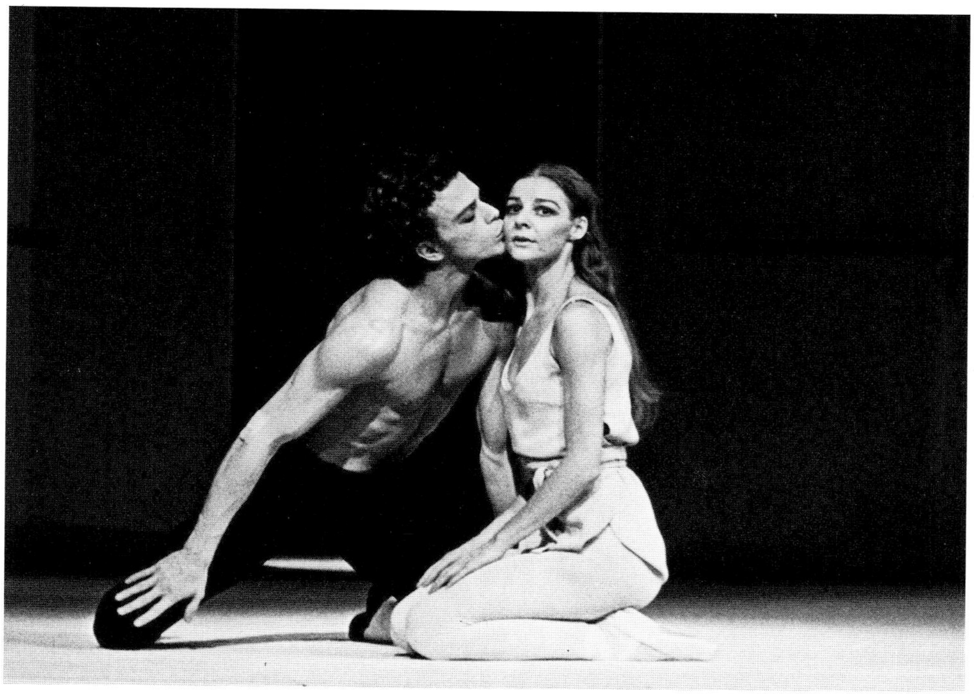

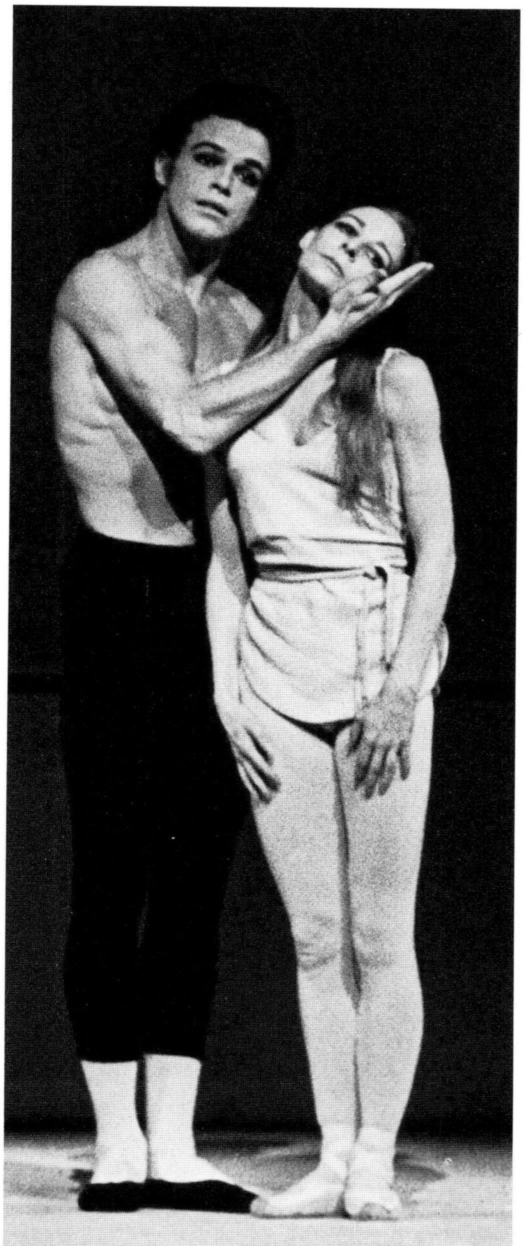

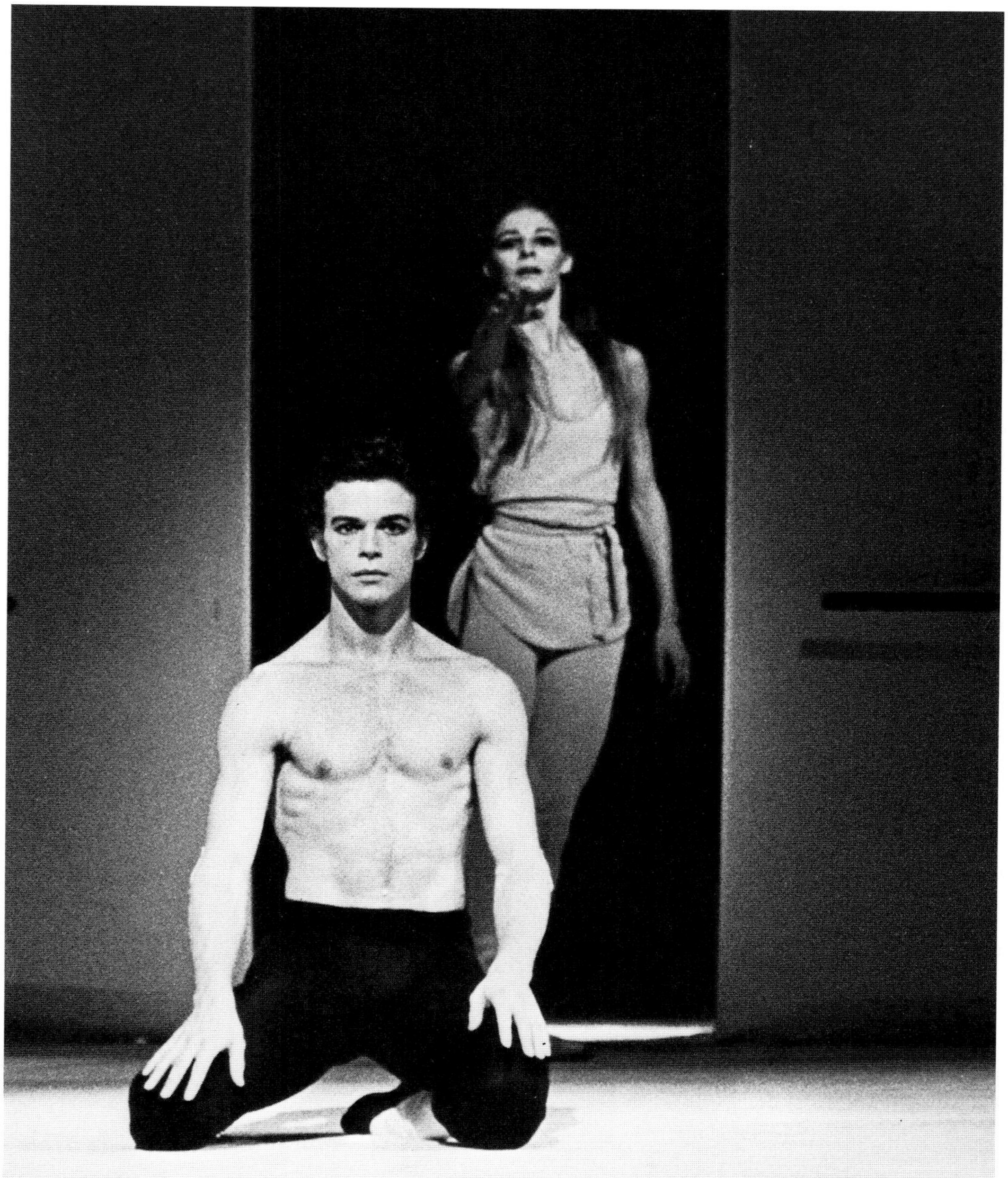

SYMPHONIC VARIATIONS

Above, with Ann Jenner, Jennifer Penney and Anthony Dowell

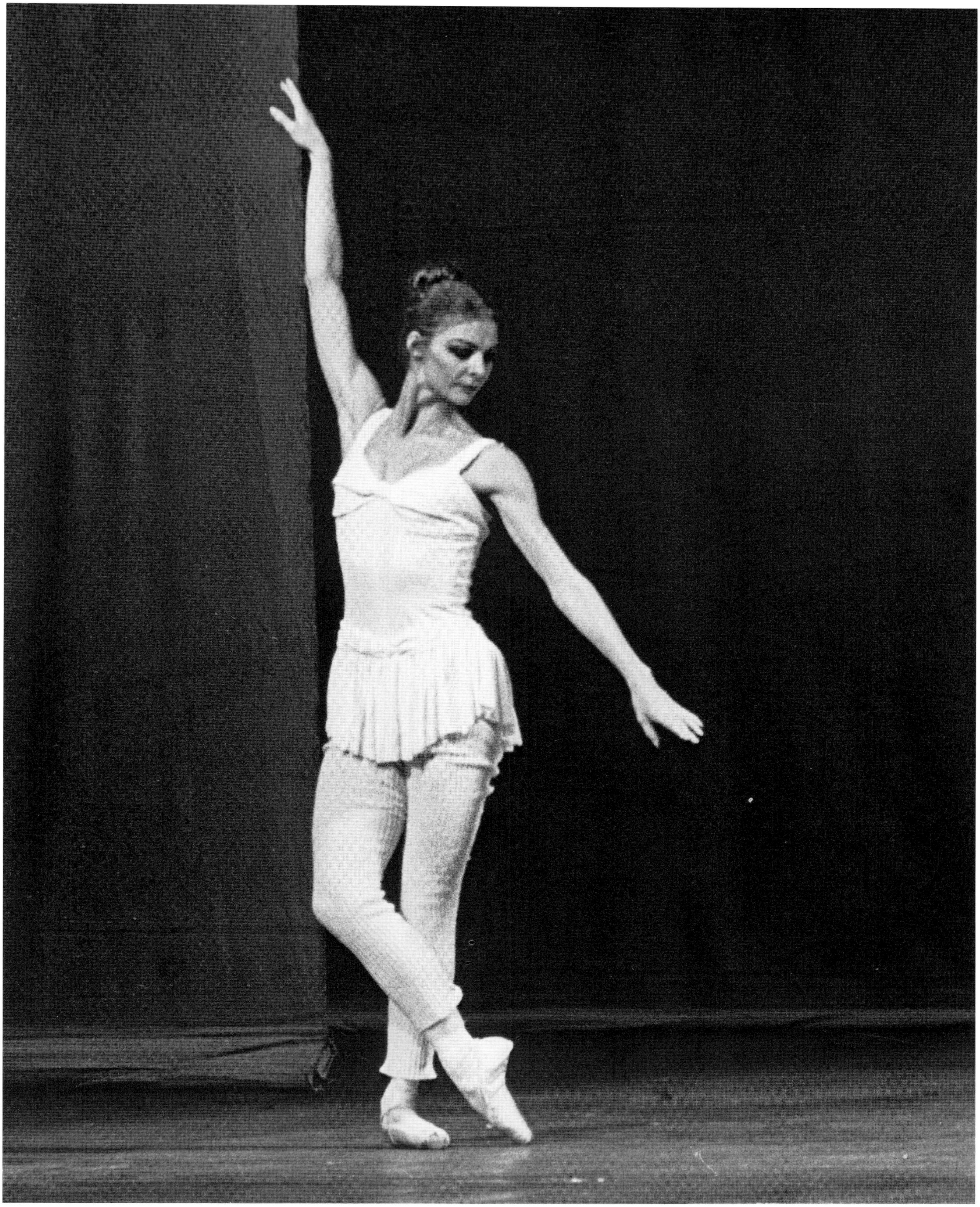

SYMPHONIC VARIATIONS

With Anthony Dowell

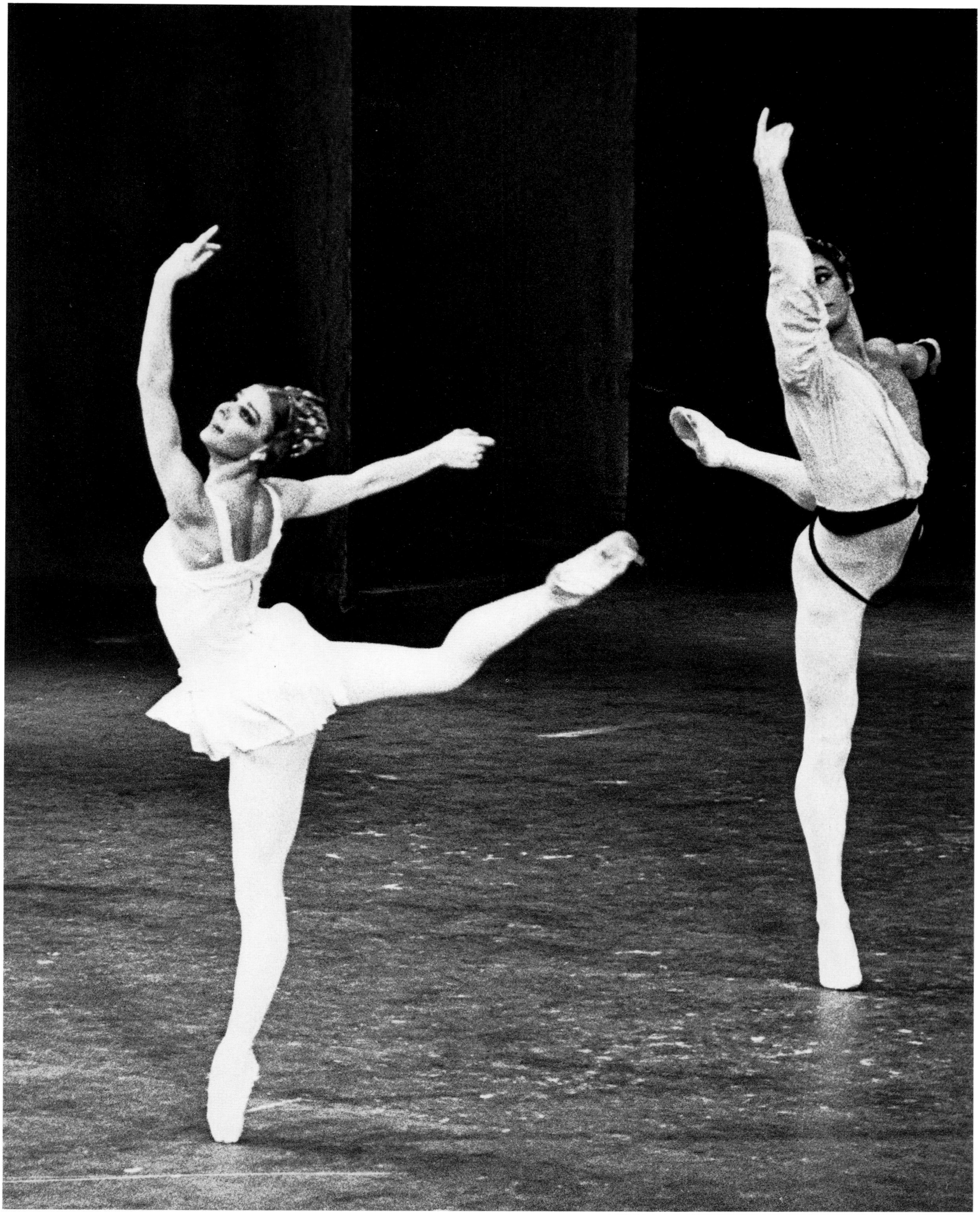

102

ions # THAÏS

With Anthony Dowell

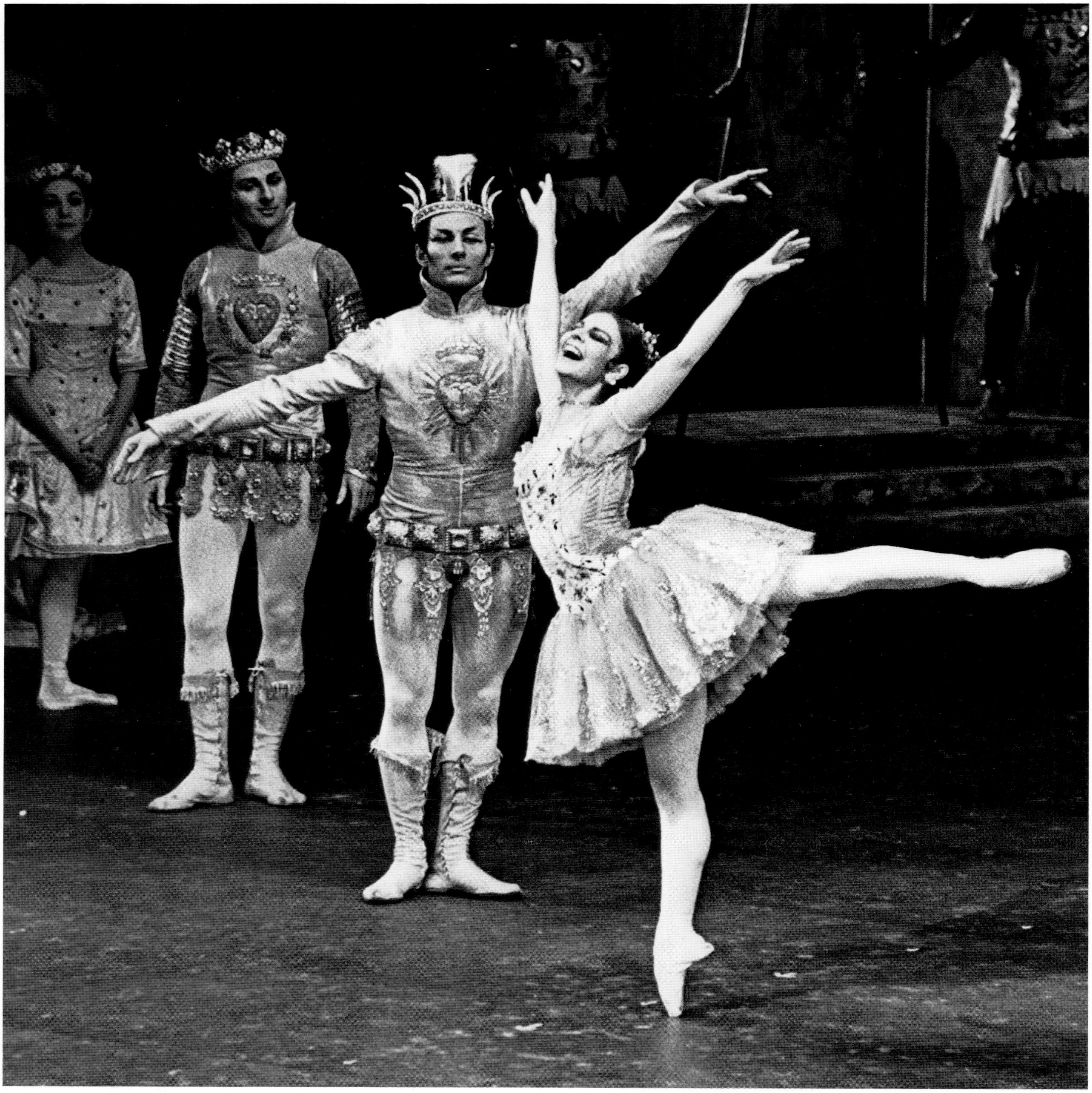

SLEEPING BEAUTY

Opposite, with Keith Rosson and David Drew.
Below, with Adrian Grater.

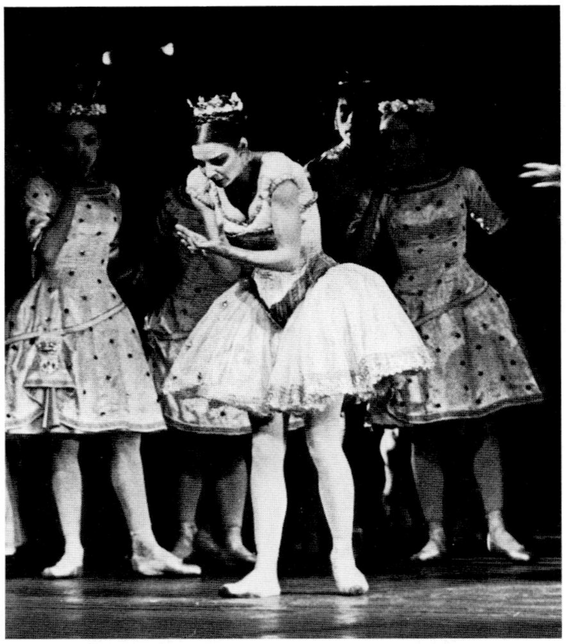

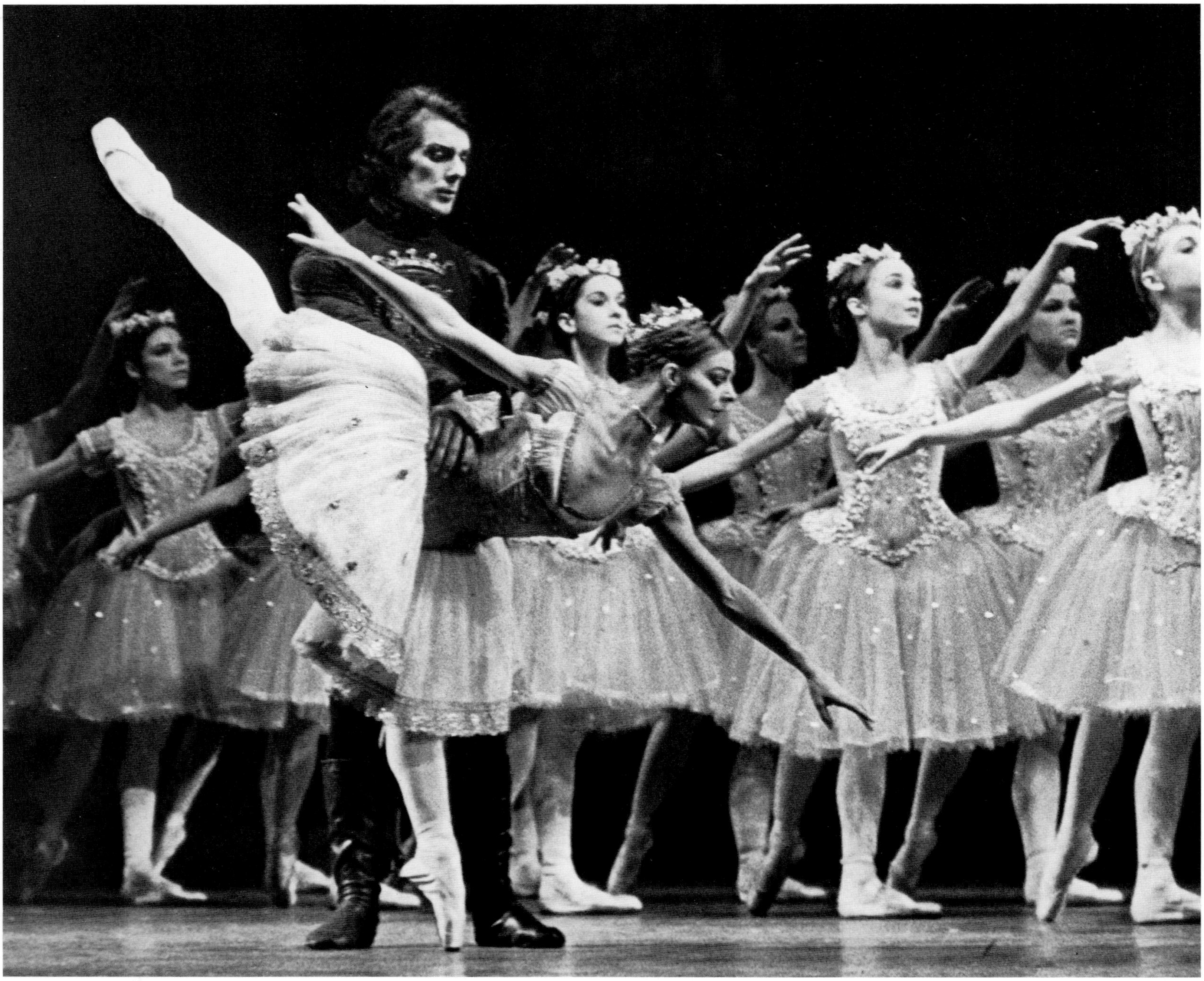

SLEEPING BEAUTY

Opposite, with Donald MacLeary.
Above, with Deanne Bergsma.

108

SLEEPING BEAUTY

Opposite, with Anthony Dowell.
Above left, with Anthony Dowell.
Above right and below, with Donald
MacLeary.

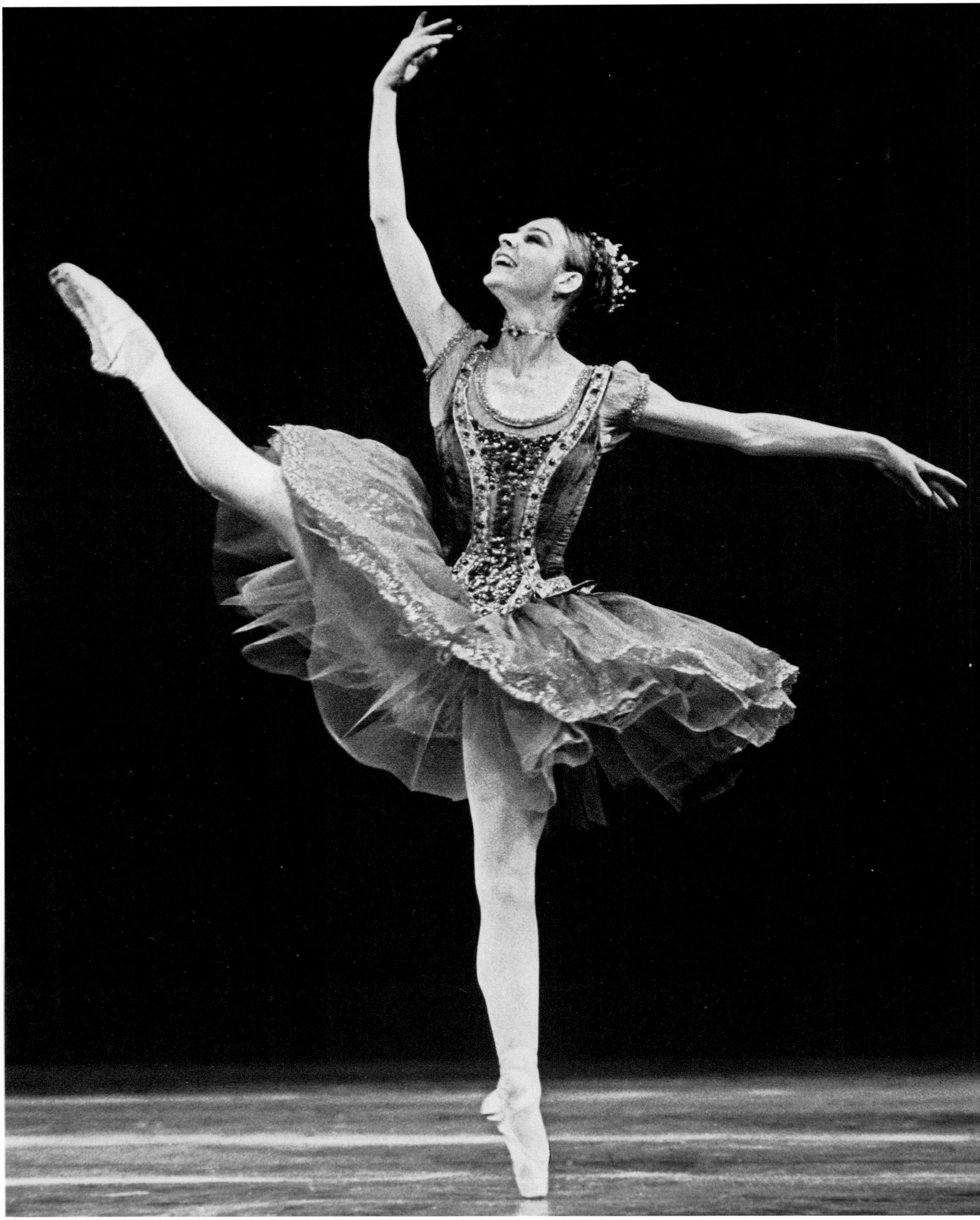

SLEEPING BEAUTY

With Anthony Dowell

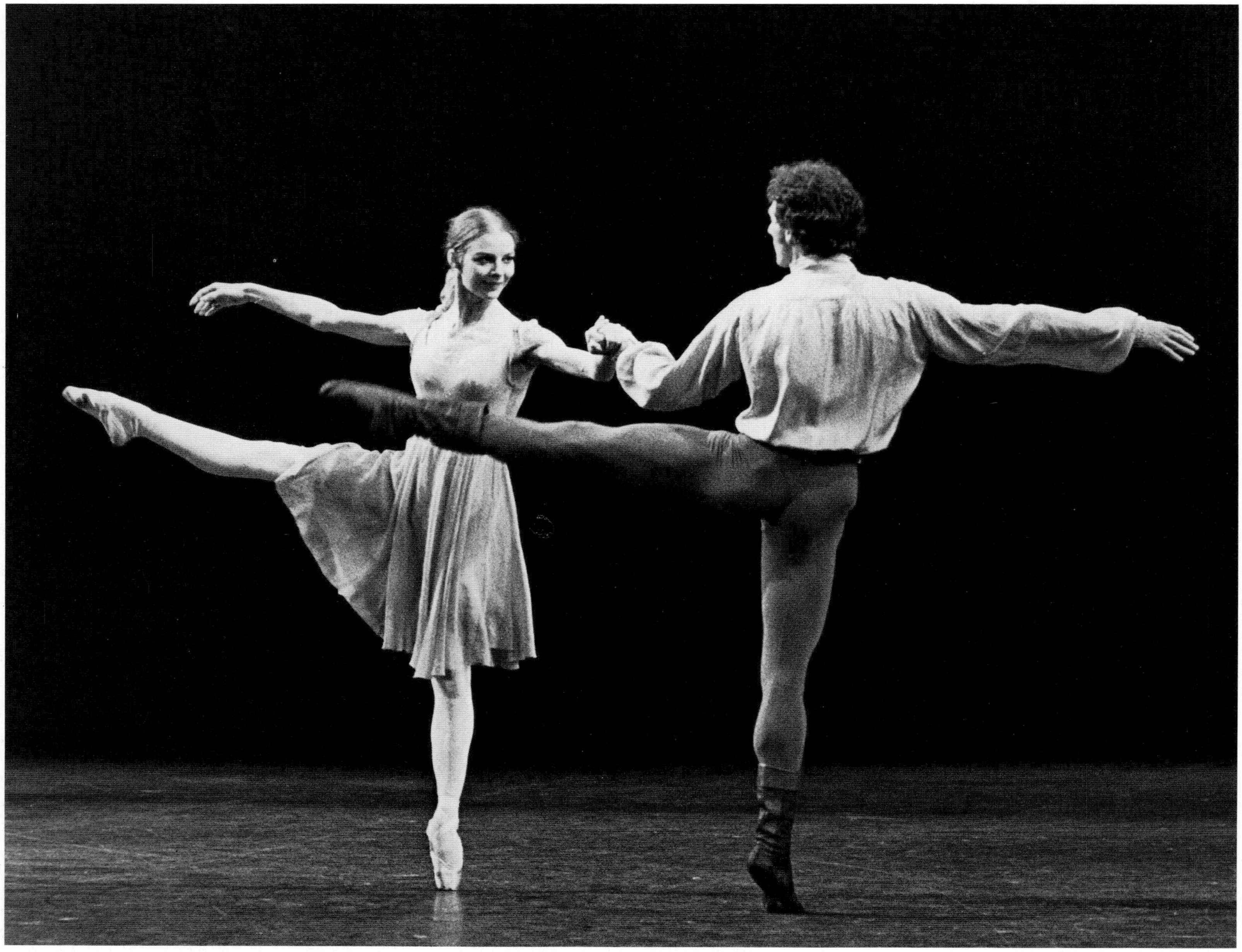

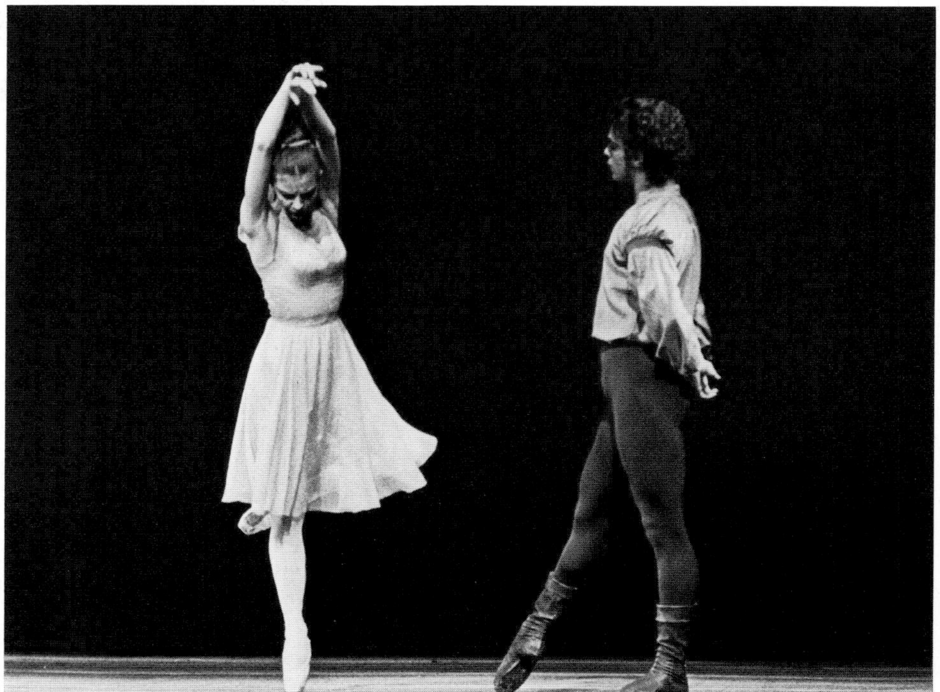

DANCES AT A GATHERING

Opposite top, with Michael Coleman.
Opposite bottom, with Anthony Dowell.
Right, with Rudolf Nureyev.

DANCES AT A GATHERING

Above, with Lynn Seymour and Laura Connor.
Left, with Anthony Dowell.
Opposite, with Anthony Dowell.

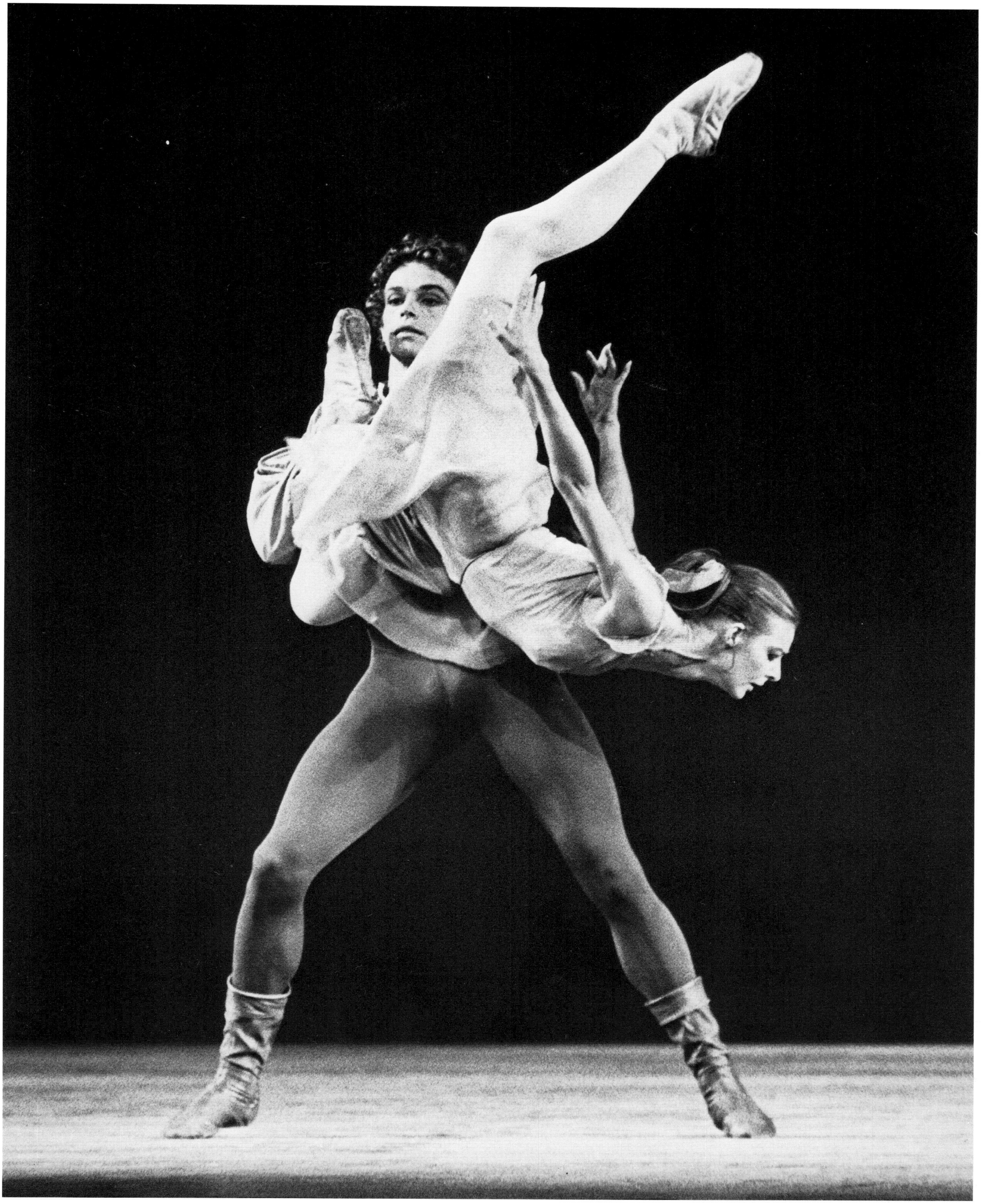

DANCES AT A GATHERING

Top, with Michael Coleman.
Below, with Rudolf Nureyev.
Opposite, with Anthony Dowell.

117

MANON

Below, with David Wall.
Opposite top, with Leslie Edwards, Derek Rencher, David Wall and Gerd Larsen.
Opposite bottom, with Anthony Dowell

119

MANON

Top, with Anthony Dowell.
Below, with David Wall and Derek Rencher.
Opposite, with David Wall.

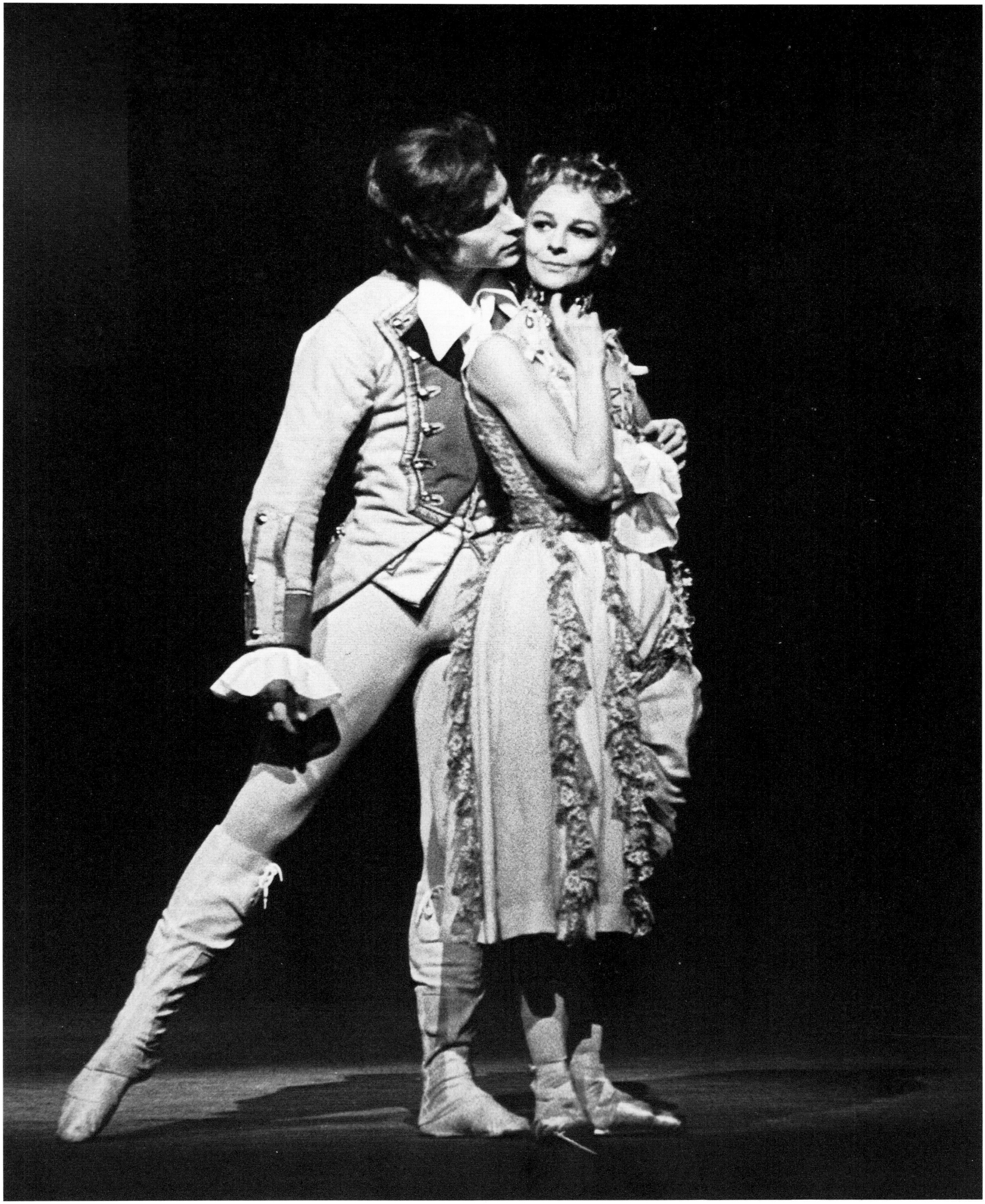

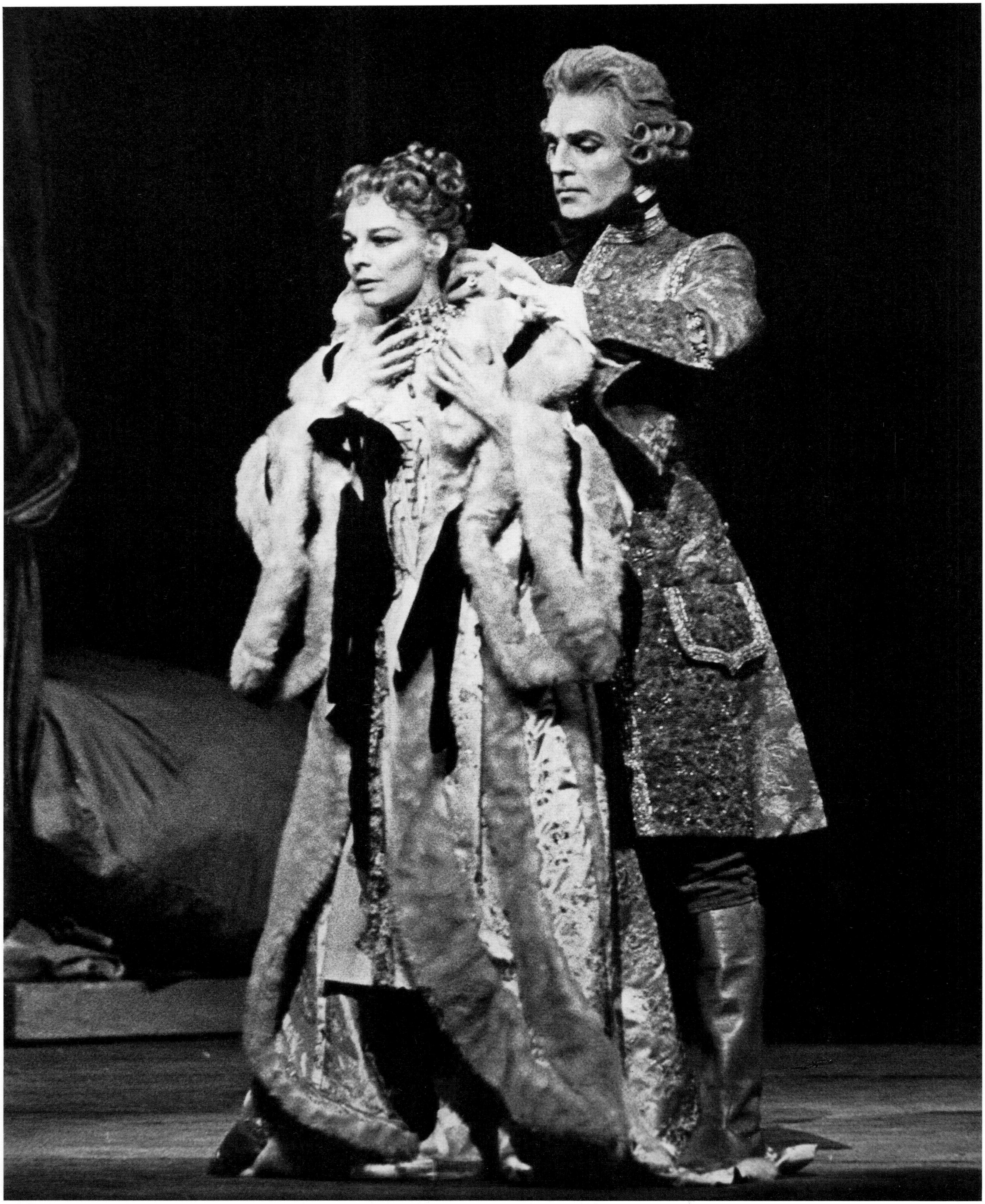

MANON

Opposite, with Derek Rencher. Above and right, with Anthony Dowell.

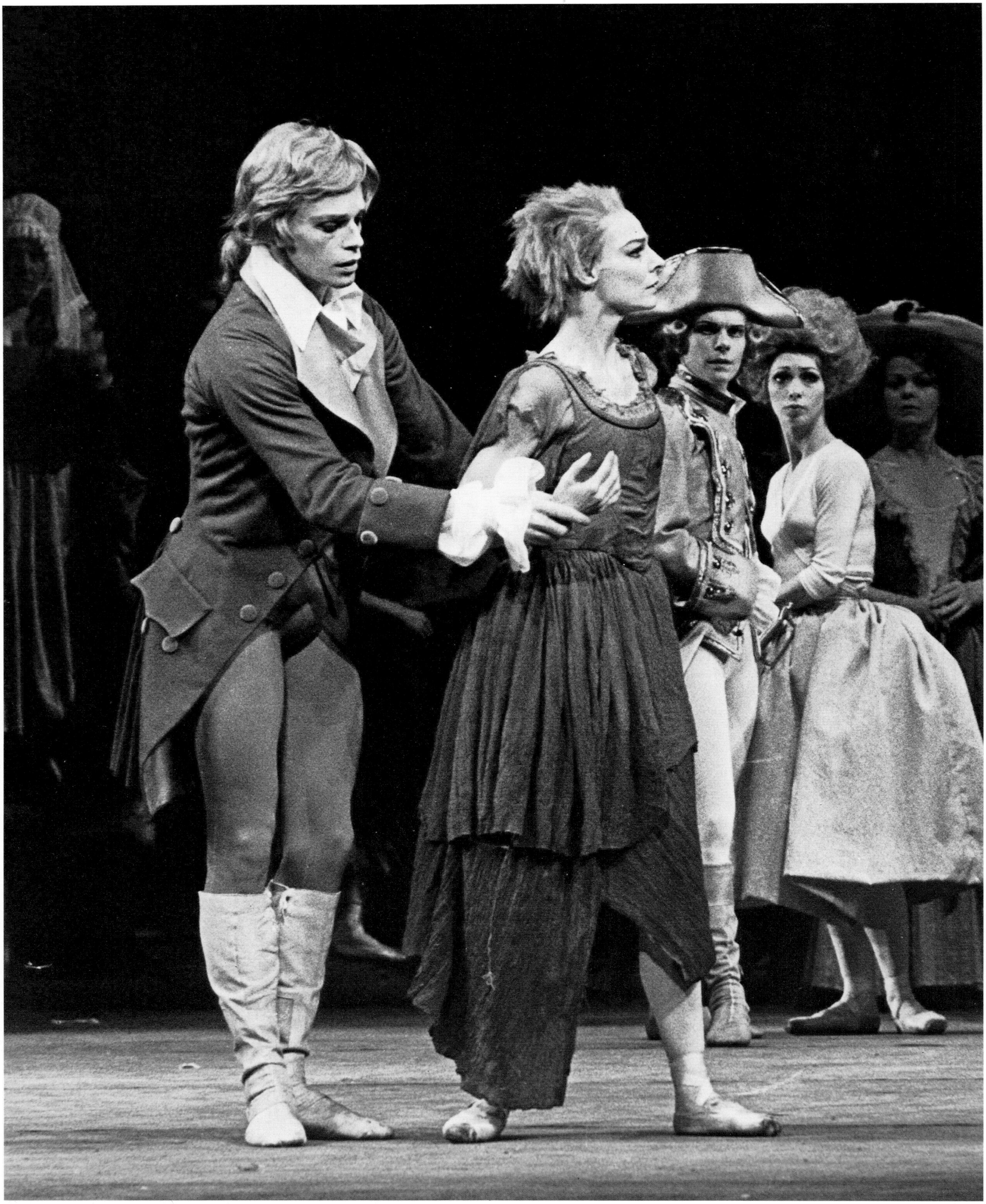

MANON

Opposite, with Anthony Dowell.
Right, with David Drew.

MANON

With Anthony Dowell

Opposite
SOUPIRS

With Anthony Dowell

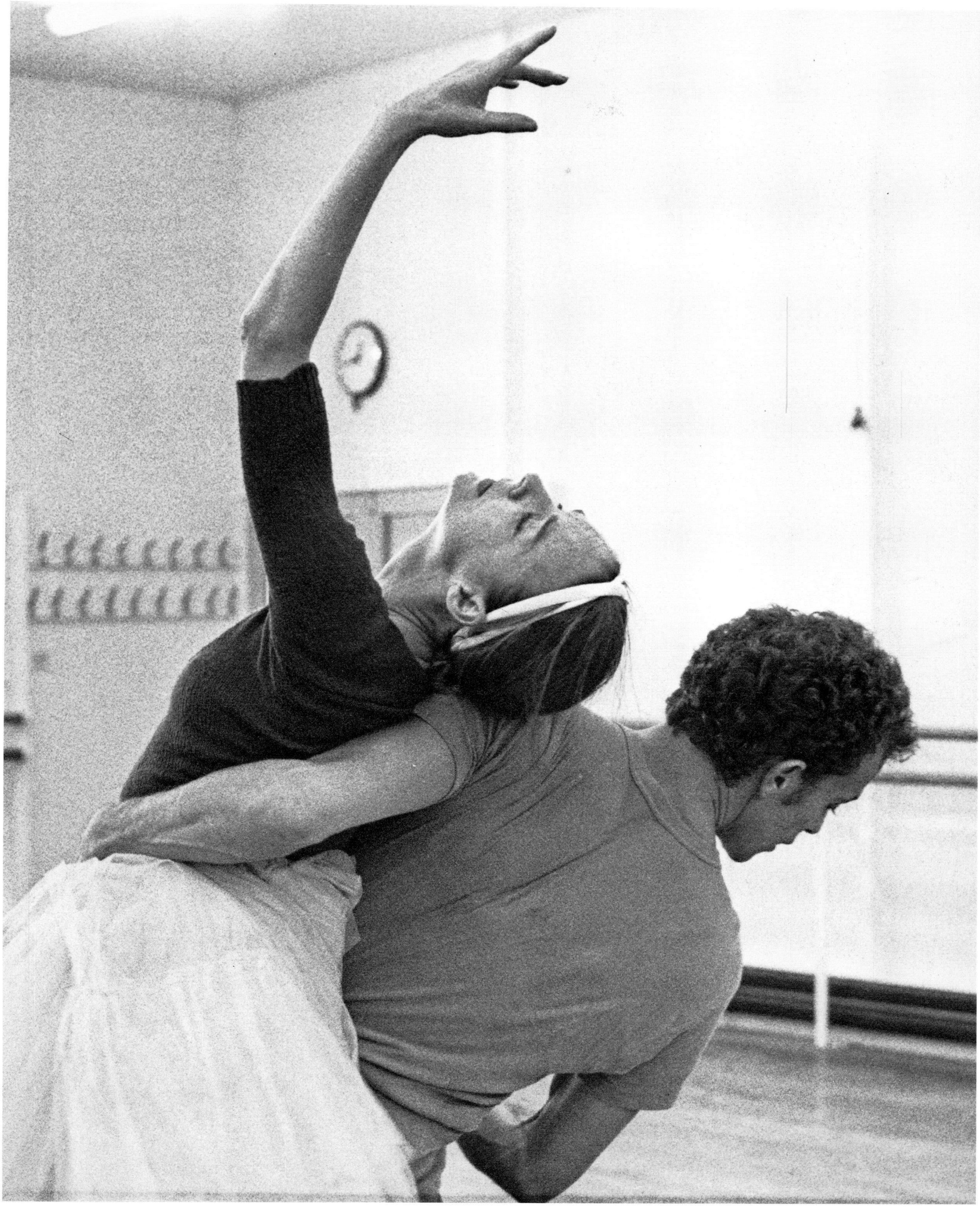

DATE DUE			
APR 26 1985			
261-2500			Printed in USA